Charles
The Story of a Friendship

Michael Joseph

Ashford Press Publishing
Southampton
1989

First published in 1943 by Michael Joseph Ltd

This edition published in 1989 by Ashford Press Publishing,
1 Church Road, Shedfield, Hampshire SO3 2HW

British Library Cataloguing in Publication Data
Joseph Michael, 1897 – 1958
Charles
1. Pets : Cats – Personal observations
I. Title
636.8'0092'4

ISBN 1-85253-050-2

Designed and typeset in 10pt Palatino by Jordan and Jordan,
Fareham, Hampshire, England.

Printed by Hartnolls Limited, Bodmin, Cornwall, England.

Contents

Introduction

In *Charles: The Story of a Friendship* Michael Joseph describes the quite remarkable experiences he shared with one Charles O'Malley over a period of thirteen years. Apart from occasional trips abroad (always anticipated and much resented by Charles), the author was seldom parted from his devoted cat. During the Second World War Charles found himself a much-admired member of the battalion, often occupying the sergeant-major's chair nearest the fire, and enjoying the valuable friendship of the author's batman. Did Charles like fish? Fish was obtained. Tender, lean steak? A clean blanket? More coal on the fire?

We ourselves have been similarly won over by the very special attributes of Siamese cats: one of our favourites was handsome Mr. Moto – he was affectionate and tolerant towards a tiresome three-year-old, delighted in travelling on his master's shoulders in the car, but was not averse to dishing out the odd swipe of the paw to any passer-by who dared to treat him as an ordinary cat. We often envisage publishers as 'lofty intellectuals', whose lives are dominated by an all-consuming interest in literature in its many and varied forms. It is therefore refreshing to discover the author –

and world-famous publisher – to be as susceptible to the charms of four-legged furries as we are.

There can be few people who would deny the beauty of a Siamese cat. Maybe their fabulous, sinewy appearance helps them to achieve without much apparent effort what a dog, for instance, would have to work hard for. They are also the most persuasive of creatures. There is also a myth that Siamese cats display particular viciousness when they kill birds for sport. Certainly, in the case of Charles this was far from the truth – he seldom unsheathed his claws, even in the roughest of games. We are sure that even 'non-cat lovers' will be 'converted' after reading this lovely book.

Those of us who love, and have the love of animals, know what fools we are every time we let them enter our hearts, for we know that they will take a little piece away when they go. Thankfully, we go on doing it, and life would be the poorer if we did not. But every so often, maybe once in a lifetime, there is the one special companion, the mention of whom brings back a thousand memories of places, people, amusement, sadness, but above all, the sense of a true friendship.

Clive and Angela Russell-Taylor

Foreword

Authors write books for many different reasons. Their motives are various, differing in degree and kind according to their needs and temperament. Perhaps because I have a professional curiosity about the motives of authorship, I begin this book by making it clear that it is not meant to be a bid for public favour. I am, to tell the truth, writing it to please myself.

Those who know and love cats may find in it some trace of the knowledge they share with me. It is an esoteric cult, this devotion of human beings to the mysterious, graceful, independent, charming and affectionate animals who occupy a unique place in our domestic economy. Unique is the right word, for the cat who lives under our roof and sits by our fire is not a domesticated animal.

He lives with us because he chooses to do so, but he is independent of mankind. Claw and fur are kept scrupulously clean for his own private purposes and advantage: even his playfulness with a fluttering leaf or a ball of paper, or – to unreasonable human beings a less pretty sight – his pursuit and apparent torture of bird and mouse are an essential part of his determination to keep himself physically fit at all costs; to preserve himself, if need be, in the ceaseless struggle for existence.

A cat in the countryside can fend for himself. Only in pavemented cities is the homeless cat at a disadvantage, and even in such artificial and formidable surroundings he can often contrive to live without human aid.

This natural independence of the cat, with one eye, as it were, always alert to the possibility of renewing his former primitive existence, gives him the right to bestow his friendship with discrimination. Many human beings like their animal pets to display a demonstrative and almost slavish affection and to them there must be something discouraging about a cat. Even the most docile and affectionate cat never completely surrenders his independence. His friendship is not easily won: indeed it can never be won without active reciprocation. A good meal every day, a casual pat on the head and the privilege of accompanying his master when he goes out for a walk are not enough to win the devotion of a cat, or even his respect.

Yet the cat does not ask for much. It is only necessary to understand his temperament and to respect his way of life. In my experience, which I know is common to others, a cat treated with kindness and intelligence will reward his human friend with a friendship that is deep and satisfying.

It is true that there are many men and women who have never felt the need of friendship with what we call (with such careless arrogance!) 'animals'. I think they are the poorer for it. Friendship – as distinct from companionship – between man and animal can be and often is a dignified relationship. At its best it is an entirely unselfish relationship – and how many human friendships are free from the base metal of self-interest?

The attitude of man towards animals, at different times and in different countries, is significant. Let it be admitted that man is a superior creature. He is lord of creation, *homo sapiens*, made (so he claims) in God's image. Animals are inferior. Anatomically, intellectually, yes: but can it be denied that animals are capable of that unselfish love which is the soul of a relationship between two living beings?

It is to the credit of mankind that we do sometimes (not, alas, in many parts of the world) become protective and affectionate towards animals in our care. I mean something more than consideration for their welfare. It is obviously sensible to care for the health and well-being of animals that render service. To neglect a horse, a cow or a dog is foolish as well as discreditable.

But what of the animals who render little or no practical service to their human overlords?

Of all the animals man has adopted for his own use or companionship the chief objects of his affection, when it exists, are undoubtedly dogs and cats. Of dogs much has been written, and more will be written. I am not one of those cat-lovers who dislike dogs, although I am always ready to champion the cat in any of the unsatisfying and inconclusive arguments which arise from time to time between cat- and dog-lovers. It is fitting that cat-lovers should extol the virtues of their favourite, for they are in the minority.

There are people who dislike cats to the point of suffering genuine discomfort in their presence. These ailurophobes are to be pitied. There are many who are indifferent to cats. The enlightened felinophile may be forgiven for comparing them with the illiterate who are unable to appreciate the beauties of literature. It must be conceded, however, that an inborn love of cats is the best passport to an understanding of their character.

That much I can claim for myself. I have always loved cats – although never an indiscriminate admirer of all cats – and have rarely been happy without at least one cat living with me. I have even had cats with me, fortuitously, during two periods of army service. I have had large families of cats, among them many memorable personalities. I have been greatly attached to perhaps a dozen cats in the past twenty years; but of all my cats there has never been a cat like my first Siamese, Charles O'Malley.

I have often wished I were an artist, a musician or a poet, and never more so than now, for I would dearly like to have been able to paint him, to compose an elegy in his honour, or to give him life in poetry. Since I can do none of these things my tribute must be like that of Anatole France's juggler, who had no gifts to offer before the altar but his own juggler's routine skill.

So, in pedestrian prose, I will try to tell the story of Charles O'Malley.

'My desk was part of his domain'
Charles and the author

CHAPTER ONE

On a sunny Saturday afternoon in August 1930 I set out for Thames Ditton to choose a Siamese kitten.

I had for some time cherished the ambition to add a Siamese to my collection. The word collection is here used deliberately, for the reigning favourite in my household, Minna Minna Mowbray, was an enthusiastic mother. Her kittens were as charming as they were numerous and the house was usually over-populated (if a self-respecting cat-lover dare use such a disparaging word) with young cats and kittens. I found it hard to part with them at any age.

Minna Minna Mowbray, a demure and pretty tortoiseshell tabby, presided over our cat family. Minna was a small cat but a great character. She lorded it over me and my human family with an air of gracious condescension and, I regret to say, her manner was becoming noticeably more imperious with the passing of time and the arrival of each successive and admired batch of kittens.

It was time, I decided, for her to be taught a lesson. Her sense of her own importance and her apparently fixed idea that she was the source and provider of all kittens called for reprisals. With this uncharitable idea in my head I had resolved to introduce into my house a Siamese cat. What could be more dislocating to her Jehovah-like pride than the appearance of a cat so different in every way from herself and her golden, fluffy kittens, and yet so decorative in a foreign, outlandish fashion?

I admit that this unworthy notion of putting Minna's aristocratic nose out of joint was not the only reason for my decision to acquire a Siamese. I had seen and admired my friend Newman Flower's two Siamese cats. I had heard, disbelievingly, from knowledgeable people that the Siamese cat was in every way superior to other breeds. There seemed to be a mystic bond uniting all Siamese cat owners, as if the possession of a Siamese were the quintessence of felinophile joy.

Today the Siamese cat is fairly well known by sight in most parts of England, but in 1930 there were many people who had never seen one. In shape and colouring they are distinctive. They have lithe, strong bodies, covered with soft, thick, cream-coloured fur. It looks as though head, feet and tail had been dipped in liquid chocolate. Their eyes are a brilliant sapphire blue, with a decided squint. (Breeders differ about the propriety of the squint.) Their long brown tails sometimes have a curious kink. This general oddity of appearance, which is surprisingly attractive, is crowned by a piercing and much-used voice. The Siamese voice is utterly unlike that of an ordinary cat. It has treble the volume, is pitched in a higher and different key, and to the uninitiated ear is – to be truthful – a loud, discordant bellow. It is suggestive of a giant seagull mewing in considerable distress blended with the full-throated cry of an aggrieved human baby. But that is merely a first impression. The subtlety and music of a Siamese cat's voice are like some modern music, not to be appreciated by the novice.

The idea of having in my house one of these rare and magnificent creatures had attracted me more and more. With all respect to my Siamese-experienced friends I did not for one moment imagine, as the train rattled me towards Thames Ditton, that I was embarking on anything more than an amusing experiment, designed, partly at any rate, to teach my haughty Minna Minna Mowbray that she was not the only pebble on the beach.

When I first saw Charles he was about six weeks old, indistinguishable from his five brothers and sisters. The kittens (Siamese kittens, I learned, were always born nearly white) were just beginning to show faint brownish traces of their characteristic markings. There they were, six lively, squeaking, innocently blue-eyed Siamese babies milling round their mother, an elegant thoroughbred called Aouda, who crooned possessively and reassuringly as mother cats do when a stranger appears.

3

'Which one would you like?' asked Aouda's owner. How was I to know? They all looked so enchantingly alike. As I hesitated, one of the kittens detached itself from the rest and with brave curiosity ran across the room towards me. I held out my hand, gently, as one should do when greeting an animal. The kitten boldly approached, looking up at me enquiringly. I stroked his soft coat and his tiny body quivered responsively. He began to purr and rub against my hand.

I hesitated no longer. 'This,' I said, 'is my little cat.'

Sheltered from the stiff August breeze by a sheet of cardboard propped up against one side of the cat basket, the kitten waited by my side for the return train to London. I had taken with me one of the special baskets I have always used for transporting my cats: a kennel-shaped basket with a wire-netted front door. Inside, the little cat was protesting loudly and plaintively. Was he regretting the impulse which had sent him scurrying from the protective radius of his warm, familiar mother into the hands of a stranger? Was it the disturbing scent of Minna and her kittens clinging to the interior of the strange box which jolted so alarmingly when moved? Or was it the noise of the cold, unfriendly wind blowing unkindly, as railway station winds always seem to blow, along the length of the platform.

As for me, I was beginning to wonder a trifle dubiously whether it was such a good idea after all to disturb the serenity of Minna Minna Mowbray's empire. When all was said, it was not entirely Minna's fault. I had encouraged her to believe that she was the

Cat of all Cats. She had been pampered and spoiled not only by me but by my family, and by several generations of our servants. ('Are you fond of cats?' had been one of my wife's stock questions when interviewing cooks and parlourmaids, in the far-off days when one could pick and choose domestic staff.) However, there was no getting away from the unpalatable fact that Minna's manner had of late been insufferable. She visited the drawing-room when, and only when, she felt like doing so, and that was not often. Perversely she bestowed her favours on the kitchen – and no self-respecting cat-lover likes to confess that his celebrated cat has to be fetched from below stairs when visitors call to admire her.

Nor was there the slightest excuse for Minna's behaviour. It was summer and the kitchen no more comfortable than anywhere else; her meals were not served exclusively below stairs; my affection for her was undiminished. But, increase my blandishments as I might, Minna ignored them. Her displays of interest and affection were reserved for the few occasions when it was inconvenient for me to receive them. If for instance I had only twenty minutes in which to shave, have a bath and change into evening dress, Minna would honour me with a personal visit, expecting a ceremonial reception. . .

It was, of course, a game: the sort of game every dignified cat likes to play at times with her human patron. As a check to over-familiarity, an insurance against the awful fate of being 'taken for granted', the game had its uses. A period of assumed indifference would surely be followed (so I can imagine Minna persuading herself) by a renewal and an increase of my devotion.

I may have smiled to myself as I sat in the train, with the basket by my side, to think that I too could take a hand in the game. I do not remember. The compartment was fortunately empty and I was able to release my Siamese kitten and try to pacify him.

Such a funny, enchanting little thing he was! His peaky head and paws looked just as if they had been slightly singed in front of a fire. His bright blue eyes, unaccustomed to the sharply changing light which flashed through the windows of the moving train, blinked incessantly; and he raised his voice – a blend of croak and squeak, and very audible – in one continuous protest against the strange things which were happening to him.

He was not in the least afraid. Already I was accepted as a friend and protector. Between his outbursts he rubbed his head against my hand and purred bravely. But I was glad when the journey ended, as I always am when I have a cat with me, for it is easy to share their apprehension and discomfort at such times.

I was living alone in London at that time, my family – including Minna Minna Mowbray – being on holiday in Cornwall. I was to join them at the week-end, bringing the new kitten with me. What my wife thought privately about the purchase of yet another cat, with all the domestic complications involved, when bountiful providence and Minna between them were already quite evidently capable of providing us with a surfeit of kittens, I do not know. Whatever her private misgivings may have been, and I have no doubt they existed, she heroically kept them to herself and was preparing to welcome the new kitten. About the views of our small daughter, then nearly three, there was no doubt whatever. Shirley was, and always has been, extravagantly fond of cats. She is, I may say in passing, even more fond of cats than I am. Generations of cats, stray cats, neighbours' cats, cats from the next parish, not to mention our own cats, follow her about, hopefully and confidently, wherever she goes.

The promised addition of a Siamese 'tikken' to our ménage was a great event in her three-year-old calendar and I was sure of at least one enthusiastic supporter.

In the next few days I probably drew some comfort from this reflection. Perhaps because I was obliged to leave him alone for a few hours every day, the Siamese kitten was wildly excited and pleased to see me when I reappeared in the large, strange room in Earl's Court which was his temporary home. He hurled himself at my legs, claws outstretched, in a delighted effort to scramble upwards. When that amusement failed, he demonstrated with unabated zeal and kittenish ferocity that it was a trick he could perform just as well on the silk bedspread. Even better in fact, since there were no restraining hands and the bed had the kindness to stand quite still during his performance.

For those first few days I was his foster-mother, his teacher and his playmate. After the little cat's thorough inspection of the premises we settled down in the tradition of London bachelors of comfortable means. Our apartments were well furnished, our food was good, and our habits regular. We dined early and we retired early. In the morning I would push the balcony door wide open and indicate the sand-covered tray I had provided, and the little cat would obediently perform his toilet, with much subsequent scraping and shuffling. This was invariably followed by a pipe-opener: a joyous race over visible and invisible obstacles at least twice round the room. Then breakfast, for preference milk and a sardine.

Charles – I must begin to call him by his name although it was not decided on until some time later – was a delightful companion. The differences between him and ordinary kittens of his own age were already noticeable. He was strong, muscular and cheerfully aggressive. His claws were not tucked neatly away in his velvet paws like other cats'. The sharp little points always protruded even when sheathed. When he slithered along the hall floor they made a pleasant tinkling sound. Less agreeable was the trail they made on armchair covers and other household fabrics, for it did not take Charles long to discover the entertainment to be had by flinging himself up on the arm of a chair or the fold of a curtain, there to hang on by his strong little claws.

In appearance he was, of course, quite unlike the kittens to which I was accustomed. Many of Minna Minna Mowbray's kittens had the lovely orange-coloured fur of their grandmother, the famous Lady Dudley; and although both Dudley and her daughter Minna were short-haired cats, a surprisingly large proportion of

Minna's kittens were long-haired. Although I have always obstinately maintained that short-haired cats are best, being more intelligent and responsive, it must be allowed that there are few prettier creatures in the world than long-haired kittens. Minna never had an unbeautiful kitten – and she had over a hundred in all – and most of them were the softest, silkiest and prettiest kittens: the sort of kitten to delight the heart of the photographers who used to provide pictures for expensive chocolate boxes.

Charles was very different. Even as a kitten he was tough. Beneath his soft, thick fur you could feel his strong, wiry body vibrating with energy. He liked to be roughly handled: roughly, that is, by comparison with the gentle handling which most kittens like. His purr was loud and frequent, and so vigorous that it seemed to shake his whole body, just as the body of an old motor car will vibrate to the rhythm of its engine.

As if to compensate for these exhibitions of virility his fur was delicately perfumed. The scent was faint but unmistakable. When I got to know more about Siamese I discovered that all Siamese have this peculiar subtle fragrance when they are very young.

In yet another respect Charles differed from our other cats. For some obscure reason very few of our cats learned to use their voice. I do not know whether Lady Dudley's vocal chords were defective but it is a curious fact that she never uttered more than a very faint mew, and that only on rare occasions. Her daughter Minna inherited her gift of silence – for so it was uncharitably regarded in our household – and Minna's kittens in turn were nearly all incapable of speech. Rissa, her last surviving descendant, of whom I shall have more to say later in this narrative, can muster only an almost inaudible squeak. The explanation of this strange feline silence must be left to biologists. My own theory is that kittens are taught to mew by their mothers, just as human children are taught to speak by their elders; and, failing such instruction, their voices become atrophied. Be that as it may, three generations of our cats had been practically silent.

Charles, by contrast, was exceedingly vocal. He used his voice continuously and, as I have already said, the Siamese voice is in itself remarkable. It is true that as a kitten Charles did not attain the full extent of his vocal powers but even so he made a great deal of noise, and he soon made it plain that he enjoyed conversation. When I spoke he answered; if I did not begin the conversation he would. It was an amusing novelty to have a cat who responded so eagerly and audibly, although I fear not everyone appreciated the loud and unfamiliar noise he made.

It was however in his general demeanour that I chiefly noticed the difference between Charles and other cats. In those early days he was tremendously active and full of energy, much more so than the ordinarily playful kitten. It was as though he had inside him a powerful coiled spring always at tension. His favourite game, then as later, was to hide himself under a chair or bed and from that concealed starting point suddenly to hurl himself like a small furry thunderbolt at my legs. It was a game he never tired of playing and one he played, though with diminishing vigour, throughout his life. Bare feet attracted him irresistibly. My attempts to undress at night were constantly impeded by efforts to escape Charles's playful rushes. However vigilant I was, he usually succeeded in scoring at least one try on my vulnerable toes. In the end I outwitted him by keeping on shoes and socks as long as possible.

From the bedroom he would follow me into the bathroom, watching with intent interest the things I did with taps. Running water fascinated him, as it does most cats. When he was very young he did not mind being splashed; and he used to sit on the edge of the bath, at the tap end where there was plenty of seating accommodation, and watch with absorbed attention and a tentatively extended paw while I took my bath.

Charles clearly found life a gay adventure. Although it is thirteen years ago I still have a vivid recollection of his high spirits and love of mischief in those early days. He would attempt incredible feats of jumping, relying, not always successfully, on the holding powers of his powerful claws as he leaped from chair to chair and from the floor to halfway up the long curtains of the french windows. I can see and hear him now, as he skidded joyously along polished wooden floors.

He had no respect for me in those days. In his eagerness to see what I had in my hand he once jumped straight at a tea cup and more by good fortune than skillful manoeuvre just escaped being drenched by hot tea. My other cats got their way by gentle insinuation. That was an art Charles learned to cultivate later. At first he made a bee-line for everything he wanted, and his curiosity was insatiable. As for his clumsiness, that was comical, although I tried hard to hide my amusement, knowing that no cat likes being laughed at.

Everyone with experience of cats knows how skillful they are at jumping on to tables and mantelpieces crowded with odds and ends, even though they cannot see them when they begin their jump. Charles had no such skill. Every jump he made was fraught with danger to property and after he had knocked over sundry pieces of valuable glass and china I had to put everything breakable out of his reach. And he was ridiculously proud of his ability to knock things over, to judge by the satisfied expression on his funny little face. Only when a pile of heavy books nearly cascaded on top of him as a result of his efforts to dislodge them did he show any sign of dismay. After two subdued minutes behind a curtain he was at his tricks again.

All this liveliness gave him a huge appetite. He ate with great gusto, gulping his food down more like a puppy than a cat. In later years he became more fastidious but as a kitten he could not eat fast enough and I had to restrain him for fear of accidents. I also took care to see that he had food which was suitable for his inexperienced stomach. The sardines which he loved proved too rich and I had to cut down his portion. I was having all my meals out at the time and except for milk, which was delivered to the flat every morning, I had to bring home Charles's food each afternoon. The problem was solved with the co-operation of my favourite restaurant; and I proudly carried back to

Earl's Court grilled fillets of sole, breast of roast chicken, cream and other delicacies; including on one occasion, I remember, the best part of a duck *à la presse*, most of which I ate myself.

He adapted himself very readily to the routine of our temporary stay in Earl's Court. I usually found him asleep on my return to the flat, but he was soon awake and ready to entertain and to be entertained. At night, when the last game had been played, he settled down happily on the end of my bed, refusing to sleep in the blanket-lined travelling basket. That basket was to him always a symbol of change and upheaval and although he would condescend from time to time to inspect it he regarded it with obvious disfavour. Even in his very early days he knew what he wanted.

It must have been lonely for him at Earl's Court for I had to be out most of the day, but whenever I could I returned early, not only to feed my little cat but to keep him company. And in so doing I was unconsciously laying the foundation of a friendship that was to last for nearly thirteen years.

CHAPTER TWO

On the long train journey to Cornwall Charles was unexpectedly docile. Already he seemed to have made up his mind that he was in safe hands; or it may be that he philosophically accepted the discomforts of travel as an inescapable feature of his new life.

I did what I could to ease the journey for him. The basket had been cleaned out, a fresh strip of blanket had been put in and folded up around the sides to protect him against draughts. I took a saucer and a bottle of milk and a few dry biscuits, for which he had already shown a great liking. There was also a slice of cold grilled sole. 'A present for the leetle cat,' said the amused *maître d'hôtel* when I lunched at his restaurant on the previous day.

Best of all, from Charles's point of view, he had room to move about inside the basket, which was big enough for a small dog. (It had in fact been sold to me as a dog basket: I have never liked the tiny hampers which are commonly used as cat baskets.) After I had coaxed Charles into it and shut the wire door he amused himself by thrusting a sturdy pale-brown paw through the wire in a painstaking effort to undo the latch. This being impossible, he contented himself with pushing an inquisitive nose against the wire, eager to see what was happening. All this was accompanied by a clamorous noise which continued all the way to Paddington. But once in the train he settled down to sleep.

In my preoccupation with his welfare I omitted to buy a ticket for him and his led to an amusing incident on the train. When the ticket collector came round Charles was having an after-lunch sleep on my knee. The ticket collector inspected him with close interest. I hastily mentioned that I had forgotten to buy a ticket for him. The collector thumbed a small book.

'He'd best travel free,' he said. 'Can't find any set charge for marmosets.'

My family were spending their summer holiday at Fowey, a favourite place with us at that time. I had written to them about Charles, giving a full account of his doings, omitting however any reference to his disconcerting fierceness. I thought that would be a nice surprise for them.

Charles was not at all embarrassed by the enthusiastic welcome he received. Refreshed by his long hours of sleep in the train he was now wide awake and full of mischief.

He surveyed the furnished house we had taken as though it had always belonged to him. I took the precaution of removing to safety all small breakable objects and some large ones, but Charles was not aggrieved. Polished floors and rugs might have been provided for his exclusive entertainment and he rushed from one corner to another, greatly alarming my wife's mother, who was ill at ease with cats at the best of times. To her Charles, with his unfamiliar appearance and strident voice, was quite terrifying.

'He's more like a young bull than a cat,' she declared. And for a long time afterwards she always referred to Charles as the bull. Charles for his part was cheerfully indifferent to such insults. Some years later my mother-in-law admitted that Charles was the only cat she ever grew to like, and that was one of the greatest compliments ever paid him.

His first visit to the seaside provided Charles with many new experiences, nearly all of them to his liking. There was, for instance, an exciting game with prawns. He soon discovered how to fish live prawns out of a bucket of sea water, and his antics with prawns, shrimps and small fishes collected from rocky pools on the beach were most diverting. Having ejected the unfortunate creature by means of a paw gingerly inserted into the bucket, he would prod it into motion all over the balcony which ran in front of the house, prancing after it and all round it with sheer delight. This pastime would continue until some kind-hearted person came to the rescue of his victim and restored it to the bucket and thence back to the pools where it belonged.

The sea frightened him at first but he soon accepted it as one of the many phenomena to be henceforth associated with human beings. There were other strange things, less terrifying but just as mysterious: like mirrors, cameras, pianos, wireless sets and other instruments which produced queer noises. I never tire of observing the reactions of kittens to such experiences.

Like most cats Charles was at first completely taken in when he saw his reflection in a mirror. He stared unbelievingly at the Siamese kitten who stared back at him. He warily approached the intruder, then stopped dead. His mystified expression when the other cat did exactly the same thing was most amusing. He blinked, put his head on one side, never taking his eyes off his reflection. Then, as if making up his mind that such an unaccountable duplication of his movements called for investigation, he cautiously went right up to the mirror. An exploratory paw was stretched out, then thrust behind the glass. Nothing there! No other cat, anyhow.

That was enough. He took one more look at himself in the glass and walked away. Evidently he was satisfied that mirrors were just one more human curiosity. He was never again deceived and ignored all attempts to interest him in his own reflection.

His interest in pianos, however, was more lasting. He showed more curiosity than alarm when he first heard a piano played, and on finding that he could himself make a satisfying noise by jumping on to the keyboard he appeared to be immensely gratified. I think it wrong however to assume it is the resulting sound which attracts so many cats to the keys of a piano. It may be merely the enjoyable sensation of the keys moving under the weight of their paws.

The attentive reader will have observed that I have so far said nothing about Charles's introduction to Minna Minna Mowbray: and indeed I have to confess that it was an anti-climax. The two cats were introduced with ceremony, and some misgiving, before the assembled family. Charles at once made a friendly dash at Minna who spat tersely and then, recovering her dignity, turned her back on Charles as if he had ceased to exist. Charles blinked his blue eyes and scampered off in another direction. As for Minna, that haughty lady gave me a look which plainly said, 'We are not amused.'

As time went on Minna and Charles settled down amicably enough. Perhaps it would be more accurate to say that a state of benevolent neutrality existed. Minna patronized Charles, but no more than she patronized any other cat or person of her acquaintance. Only when her kittens were very young did she warn Charles off, and that she did very sharply. Charles's only retaliation was to swear disgustedly at the kittens when they got in his way but he prudently kept out of reach of Minna's formidable claws. She was a small cat, as I have said, but a demon in any sort of fight.

Our London home in 1930 was in the neighbourhood of Regent's Park. When we all came back from Fowey many new experiences awaited the little Siamese cat. For the first time there was a garden to be explored: not much of a garden from our point of view but an ideal playground for Charles and other cats. The few flowers that were with difficulty persuaded to grow in its inhospitable soil were no doubt impressive to a small kitten and the thick bushes and other greenery provided satisfying lairs and hiding places. Charles amused himself as all kittens do; lying stealthily in wait in the vain hope of trapping the dancing butterflies between his suddenly outflung paws. At this pastime and the more reprehensible one (as we choose to regard it) of stalking birds, Charles, I am glad to say, was nearly always unsuccessful. Minna and her family could beat Charles pointless when it came to hunting of any kind and I dare say they had many a good feline laugh at his expense. Poor Charles never gave up trying, at any rate while he was a kitten. He scowled hard at the elusive butterflies and birds and his little jaw chattered away in fierce silence, but the results were negligible.

I do not record this to his credit – and indeed it is nonsense for us humans to expect a cat or any other animal of primitive instincts to conform to an arbitrary notion of what is right and wrong. You can teach a dog not to steal food or chase rabbits. A cat is different. He does not acknowledge human laws and standards. Obedience to our code may be useful and flattering but to be obedient an animal must sacrifice his independence: and that, for some of us at least, is an indispensable part of a cat's charm.

Soon after we returned to London the question of Charles's name was finally settled. This important matter was debated by all members of the family. The naming of our pets is always a serious responsibility, not to be lightly undertaken.

It occurs to me as I write this that the naming of cats is an almost infallible guide to the degree of affection bestowed on a cat. Perhaps not affection so much as true appreciation of feline character. You may be reasonably sure when you meet a cat called Ginger or Nigger or merely Puss that his or her owner has insufficient respect for his cat. Such plebeian and unimaginative names are not given to cats by true cat-lovers. There is a world of difference between the commonplace 'Tibby' and the dignified and sonorous 'Tabitha Longclaws Tiddleywinks' which the poet Hood christened his cat. And her three kittens called Pepperpot, Scratchaway and Sootikins reveal an affectionate interest which is never displayed by such ordinary names as Sandy or Micky.

We cannot all rise, of course, to Southey's heights. He, you may remember, called his cat 'the most noble the Archduke Rumpelstiltzchen, Marcus Macbum, Earl Tomlefnagne, Baron Raticide, Waowhler and Scratch.' When summoning His Excellency to a saucer of milk, no doubt 'Rumpel' sufficed, but Southey undoubtedly had the right idea.

Not that grandiloquent or fancy titles are necessary to a true appreciation of cats. What could be more dignified or appropriate than the name of Doctor Johnson's cat Hodge? And the handsome Bedfordshire cat who is mentioned later in this story is admirably suited by his name of Albert. Without doubt the names given to individual cats shed interesting light on their human owners. No one but a true cat-lover could call his cat Gilderoy, Absalom, Potiphar, Wotan, Feathers or Shah de Perse.

It may be thought that such elegant names are

difficult to live up to, and it is true that in ordinary usage even the most fervent cat-lover will use a convenient abbreviation. But I am sure every true lover of cats will agree that there are times when nothing less than full ceremonial titles will serve.

But I must return to Charles O'Malley. And this is surely the right moment to inform the reader that such was his registered name. It was not my idea. I was lunching with Charles Graves, to whom I explained that I wanted something quite unoriental for my amusing, mischievous little cat. 'Why not Charles O'Malley, the Irish Dragoon?' he said. So Charles O'Malley (without the Irish Dragoon, for that would have been too fanciful) it was.

In course of time such variations of his name as Charley-Boy came to be used. It is one of our family idiosyncrasies to change the names of our pets from time to time and Charles was no exception. He had to endure many and various terms of endearment during his long life. But some of them would look ridiculous in print and I will not catalogue them. I must however mention the name on his collar. The silver disc carried my surname and address and to many neighbours Charles was consequently known as Joseph. Years later, when Charles and I were temporarily alone in London, the daily woman who used to 'do' for me must have wondered why I gave her a strange look when she entered my bedroom one morning with a cup of tea and seeing Charles asleep on my bed greeted me (as I thought for one embarrassed moment) with a cry of 'Joseph, darling!'

But let me return to our Regent's Park garden. Here Charles discovered for the first time the existence of other people's cats. Strange, unfriendly cats they must have seemed to him as they inspected him warily. All the cats of the neighbourhood – and anyone who has lived near Regent's Park knows that cats abound there – showed a lively interest in Charles. They gathered round him as though he were a piccaninny in a school of white children; sniffing, probing, spitting, snarling – and, worst of all, laughing at him. I watched the performance many times from my window and am convinced they did laugh at him. Poor little Charles! He was so ready to be friends, but they would have nothing to do with him.

If you have ever seen a solitary country bird being set upon by a pack of town sparrows you will sympathize, as I did, with Charles. Many times I rescued him from the unwelcome attentions of other cats. His timorous attitude surprised me a little, for I had never known a timid kitten. All Minna's family were sturdily defiant of everything from the day their eyes opened. Siamese cats, I had often heard, were more pugnacious than most but there was no sign of pugnacity in Charles. And as time went on he confirmed my first impression. To be truthful – as I must in writing about him – he was a gentle cat.

Even in self-defence, at which nearly all cats are adept, he was inefficient. He had no relish for a fight and would always avoid trouble if he could. Perhaps that was why Minna Minna Mowbray was so surprisingly tolerant of him. They made an amusing contrast when Charles was a full-grown cat. He then looked, to the casual eye, as ferocious and sinister as a prize-fighter, while Minna, with her soft little body, her demure expression and innocent amber eyes, looked incapable of protecting herself, let alone causing any trouble. Yet it was Minna who attacked a neighbouring bull terrier with such ferocity that its owner entered a mild protest. And if two cats were seen or heard streaking across our garden, one in snarling pursuit of the other, you could be reasonably sure that the cat in front was Charles.

With the departure of summer Charles spent more and more time indoors. There he was safe, not only from other cats but from the chilly winds of autumn. He showed early in his life an intense dislike of cold. Before winter had fully set in he was always to be found in the warmest corners of the house. His favourite place was under the kitchen stove, where he seemed unmindful of the danger of live embers dropping on top of him. I was horrified when I came home one day and found a large burnt patch of fur on his back, and astonished to hear that a strong smell of singeing had led to his rescue. Charles loved the warmth of fire too much ever to dread it and on many occasions he singed his tail or his fur as a result of sitting too close to open fires or electric stoves.

In that first winter his coat became prematurely dark. As a rule Siamese cats retain until fairly late in life the unblemished cream colour which contrasts so decoratively with the seal-brown of their mask-like face and their feet and tail. As if to compensate for the brownish tinge which spread along his back – although it was too slight to be regarded as even a minor disfigurement – Charles went through no 'ugly duckling' stage. Most cats, when they grow out of kittenhood, pass through a gawky phase. Charles, even in the eyes of unprejudiced outsiders, emerged from kittenhood with honours. He was, as a young cat, one of the most graceful creatures I have ever seen.

At play he was a delight to watch. One of his earliest toys was a ping-pong ball. Most of the cats I have known like playing with these light celluloid balls and Charles excelled in enthusiasm if not in skill. From one side of the room to the other he would hurl himself after the elusive ball and when it bounced away at unexpected angles his acrobatics in mid-air were an endless source of amusement. He did not seem to mind being laughed at during these performances, and I believe he really saw the humorous side of it himself.

With certain other playthings he was more intent. An unfailing temptation to cats of all ages is a fair-sized feather tied to a piece of string and dangled before them; and a more amusing effect is obtained by inserting a small length of elastic. Thus reinforced the string can be attached to a door handle, and if the feather hangs about eighteen inches from the ground a cat will eagerly play with it. I soon found that anything with a feather induced a more purposeful onslaught in Charles. It was the same with the toys I sometimes bought him on Bank Holidays. We lived near Gloucester Gate, and on Bank Holidays there was always a crowd of people streaming up from Camden Town towards the Zoo. Vendors of horribly yellow lemonade and toys for the children did a flourishing trade; and among the toys to be had for a penny was a highly coloured representation of a bird with feathers in its tail. This was attached by a yard or so of twine to a thin bamboo cane, and when you twirled it round the stick the tail feathers of the bird ingeniously revolved, making at the same time a loud, whirring sound.

This toy excited Charles enormously, and it never lost its fascination for him. The prodigious leaps he made in pursuit of the spinning bird! His jaws chattered in realistic snarls and his tail lashed furiously. Eventually of course he managed to get his claws into the dummy bird and, unlike Minna, who would walk away with an air of offended dignity as soon as she discovered a deception of this sort, he would tear the stuffing out and scatter it all over the floor.

It was not long before his claws were doing other damage in the house. The stair carpets received special attention. My wife was soon in despair and did not seem at all pleased when I pointed out that we could get another carpet but not another Charles. However, I did my duty by loudly scolding Charles every time I caught him in the act, which was often enough. Then he would race away in simulated panic, laughing (I am convinced) as he went. But no amount of scolding cured him of the habit, and carpets exercised a permanent fascination for him all his life.

Nor were carpets the only victims of his extremely sharp claws. Chairs covers came next in order of popularity, with table legs a close third. Fortunately polished wood did not appeal to him and it was the kitchen table which received most attention. Out of doors Charles soon learned that trees could be satisfactorily scratched. This industrious habit which all cats share is not, I think, intended to sharpen their claws, as most people believe, but to clean them. I have noticed that cats often clean their claws in this manner after a meal: and that is consistent with their invariable habit of removing as soon as possible all traces of food and its smell from their fur and paws – one more instance of the cat's strict adherence to the wisdom of the jungle.

Mischievous as he was, Charles was never an aggressive cat. He was willing to play with anyone. Minna gave him a wide berth and carefully kept her kittens out of his way. Peter, my wife's wire-haired terrier, was too old to play but old enough to be tolerant of a young Siamese cat. Perhaps in his doggy wisdom he recognized canine traits in Charles: as, for instance, his pleasing habit of answering to his name. Charles always came when I called him – a breach of feline etiquette as practised by Minna and her tribe but no doubt commendable in Peter's eyes.

I think Charles would dearly have liked to join in the games which the cats of the neighbourhood played up and down the garden walls. When night came and they went out to play Charles would listen wistfully to the music of their voices. But, as I have said, they would have nothing to do with such an obvious little foreigner, and he knew better than to go where he was not wanted. For my part I was glad he did not join in their vulgar brawls. He got into enough mischief at home.

As a family we have a catholic taste in pets, each of us, children included, having his or her own favourites. Mine were always cats, and cats came first with Shirley, although from an early age she showed the liveliest affection for other animals. My wife, before I knew her, always had her own dog, and she also liked birds. Before her marriage she had had little to do with cats and I suspect she did not care very much for them. If so, she said nothing, but it was not long before her tolerance of my cats changed to affectionate interest: a conversion for which I claim no credit whatever. On my side, I cheerfully tolerated her dogs and birds. The lizards, white mice, goldfish and other juvenilia were kept more or less strictly to the nursery. I shall have more to say presently about various additions to our domestic menagerie, which no doubt gave us an odd reputation among our less animal-minded friends and acquaintances. The point I want to make now is that the animals themselves seemed to share our mutual tolerance. Occasionally Minna would survey Rupert the canary with a baleful eye; and the more adventurous of her kittens would display too active an interest in the white mice and goldfish, but no more than that. All things considered, harmony prevailed.

Until, that is, the arrival of Charles. So eager was he as a kitten to find out how everything worked that nothing within his reach was safe. I do not believe – and the evidence goes to prove it – that he would ever have seriously harmed any of the other household pets, although the white mice would no doubt have died of fright if too closely confronted by those sharp claws and squinting blue eyes. It was just insatiable curiosity and a spirit of unquenchable mischief that made it unsafe to leave him alone with smaller and defenceless animals.

Rupert was his favourite target, and I use the word target with some emphasis. Before Charles's arrival in Regent's Park Rupert lived in a handsome cage on top of a stand in the drawing-room. It did not take Charles long to find out that by projecting himself hard against the top of the stand the cage with the fluttering canary inside would overbalance; and whenever he got the chance Charles would hide himself in the drawing-room and hurl himself at the stand. It was fairly heavy but under Charles's onslaught down it would come. He never attempted to get the canary out of the cage. Perhaps it is too much to say that Rupert became accustomed to these attacks (despite the saying that eels get used to being skinned) but I do not think he was unduly alarmed. He was a remarkable bird, who suffered from rheumatism and bad temper – perhaps the two were interrelated – and would peck viciously at anyone except my wife who went up to his cage. I refuse to believe that he was greatly frightened by Charles's antics. The stand of course had to go and the cage was hung out of Charles's reach; after which he took no further notice of Rupert.

Our house in Regent's Park was built at a time when such amenities as bathrooms and central heating were not envisaged. A bathroom had been installed, but the house with its five storeys and basement was a chilly place in winter. The front door opened on to a hall, which was really a passage. This architectural device, so common to many London houses of the period, served admirably as a conductor of draughts straight up the staircase at the other end of the hall. As I have already said, Charles felt the cold acutely. If you live in a cold and draughty house and wish to see for yourself how uncomfortable it can be for a cat who has to spend most of his life a few inches from ground level, just lower your hand to where the cold air comes through the cracks between doors and floor. It was not surprising that even the hardy Minna Minna Mowbray patronized in winter the draught-proof basket which had been provided for her comfort. This stood a foot or so from the ground and made it possible for her to bask in the warmth of the drawing-room fire. A similar basket was provided for Charles, and he gratefully made use of it.

However cold the weather, and despite the attraction of this basket, Charles was nearly always to be found sitting on the draughty landing when I returned home. I can imagine his disgusted feelings when I was delayed and he sat there in vain, but I do not think this happened often, for my wife noticed that he kept an ear open for the sound of my key. As soon as he heard the familiar noise he would make for the landing, from which he had a good view of the front door. Sometimes he would run downstairs and entangle himself in my legs, but he usually waited until I picked him up on my way upstairs. He always greeted me with signs of affection and in this he was gratifyingly different from my other cats. I can remember only one other who always showed pleasure at seeing me. That was the handsome, lazy Gynaboi, one of Lady Dudley's earliest kittens, whom I described in an earlier book.

If I showed any favouritism to Charles in return for this devotion it was not in the form of caresses or special privileges. When he was young I treated him none too gently. Minna would not have tolerated for a moment the cavalier handling I gave Charles. He was a young barbarian and I treated him accordingly. To the dismay of onlookers I would throw him on to my shoulder, send him skidding across the room, turn him on his back and make him lie absolutely still (a trick which he willingly performed all his life) and even hit him hard on the back. I discovered that, far from objecting to a slap on the back near the base of his tail, he actually liked it, and would stay in the same position stiffening his body in pleasurable resistance until I was hitting him really hard with the palm of my hand. He always let me know by a squeal of protest when he had had enough, but there was no doubt about his enjoyment. As soon as it was over he would make the most extravagant gestures of affection, purring loudly and rubbing himself against me in a frenzy of pleasure.

There were however two things he did not like. One was the Hoover. Its frightening noise and appearance as it pushed its way across the carpet were enough to alarm any cat. At first however Charles was merely curious. I think he would have accepted it as yet another phenomenon if I had not playfully tried one day to clean his fur with one of the special attachments. No sooner did he feel the touch of it on his back, with its literally hair-raising effect, than he leaped a yard in the air. It was a thoughtless prank which I would not have attempted if he had not been so inquisitive. He never overcame his dislike of the hoover after that.

The other thing he disliked was being splashed with water. He still followed me into the bathroom but he was so often splashed, usually by accident but once or twice, I confess, by design that he learned to keep out of my way until I had had my bath. When the bath was emptied, however, he used to jump in and roll on his back over the still warm surface. He abandoned that habit after a time, finding it almost impossible to avoid being splashed. But he never ceased to be interested in taps, especially if they dripped conveniently into basins. The invariable sequel to fish for breakfast was an upward jump and a long drink from the trickle of water. He seldom drank water from a dish always preferring to go upstairs and drink from a washbasin.

Life in a human household has other drawbacks for cats besides vacuum cleaners and clumsy bathers. Brooms, for instance. The most kind-hearted housemaid cannot be expected to resist the temptation to push a broom at cats when they get in the way, and Charles was always getting in the way. He soon learned to keep outside the radius of an active broom.

He also hated Christmas, for that meant strange and terrifying noises. Crackers and fireworks were altogether too much for him, as they were for all our animals. Only Peter remained on the scene to bark a vigorous protest: Charles and the other cats promptly disappeared.

CHAPTER THREE

With the coming of Spring Charles renewed his interest
in the world out of doors. His pleasure at finding the
sun grow steadily warmer was plain to see. If ever
there was a sun worshipper it was Charles. He would
always choose the sunniest patch to lie in and liked
nothing better than to sprawl in the sun half asleep, his
brilliant blue eyes half closed, his graceful body
relaxed, and only the gentle movement of his long tail
to indicate that he was not really asleep.

He had now grown into a handsome young cat and
except for the early darkening of his coat was a typical
thoroughbred Siamese. He had the characteristic
marten-shaped head approved by authorities on breed-
ing, and a strong, flexible body which in motion was
strongly suggestive of his distant cousins the wild cats.
As he grew older this sinuous motion became even
more pronounced. His slim hind legs were slightly

longer than his forelegs and when he walked down stairs his body swayed from side to side like that of a tiger.

His voice was now deep and powerful, and he used it incessantly. It was, I admit, an acquired taste. Visitors hearing our Siamese for the first time could not hide their astonishment. Some thought it a dreadful noise and said so. But I would not listen to adverse criticism. After generations of silent cats it was, for me at least, a refreshing experience to own one who could use his voice.

Charles was a cat of aristocratic lineage. His great-great-grandfather was the famous Champion Bonzo and many illustrious Siamese names adorned his pedigree. I had been urged to show him, for in spite of the premature darkish tinge in his coat he conformed closely to the ideal Siamese type. I had however no experience of showing cats and preferred to give him more freedom as a pet. The life of the show cat is rigorously disciplined. Another reason influenced me. There was at that time considerable risk of infection in spite of the strict precautions taken at shows, and Siamese cats were said to be delicate, especially when young.

I had been fortunate with my cats, none of whom had ever suffered from serious ailments, and now that Charles was a year older I hoped he would escape infection, but in the early summer of 1931 he fell ill. The germs of disease strike quickly at cats and in a few hours he was plainly in a bad way. By good fortune I was advised to consult a veterinary surgeon in Maida Vale. Bryan Cartland, who was to prove a good friend to me and my cats, came round at once. He shook his head doubtfully when he examined Charles, who was already painfully weak. Gastro-enteritis was often fatal to cats, and my poor Charles was the victim of an acute attack.

No one could have been more skillful and considerate than Bryan Cartland during that critical illness. But he held out little hope of recovery, for there was no recognized cure. Charles got rapidly worse in spite of all we could do. He was kept in his basket in my dressing-room out of draughts and was so weak that he could only move with difficulty. As a last resort Cartland suggested an injection. It offered only a faint chance of recovery, but any chance was worth taking. I nursed Charles throughout that night, giving him every two hours the treatment that Cartland had prescribed. Poor little cat! He was so weak that he lay helpless on his side and his ulcerated mouth could hardly close on the tablets I had to coax him to swallow.

When morning came Cartland rang up. My wife, who answered the telephone, said he seemed surprised to hear that Charles had lived through the night. He was coming round at once. Even I could see that Charles was perceptibly better; and Cartland confirmed my rising hopes.

That illness was a milestone in my relationship with Charles. Up to that time he had been a delightful and amusing companion. Now he was much more than that. And – though this may be my fancy – his regard for me seemed to change into something deeper and more enduring. A bond had been forged between us:

from that time on he was my cat and I was his master.

I know there are people who scoff at the idea of friendship between man and beast. There may even be cat-lovers who will dispute the propriety of the word master in relation to a cat, who they will say, not without some justification, acknowledges no human master. But I do not use the word in a possessive sense. Nor do I wish to boast of Charles's devotion. The love of an animal is something to be grateful for and proud of, but it should not be paraded.

When Charles had fully recovered his strength Cartland advised castration, fearing that he might pick up some infection from other cats. Chiefly because I now had faith in Bryan Cartland's judgement (faith which was never to be misplaced) I agreed to the operation, although I had never had it performed on any of my other cats.

So Charles became without hope of posterity. Whether it was his illness, my care of him – which I am sure he understood – this operation, or just the process of growing up, his disposition seemed to change. Love of mischief remained but his juvenile boisterousness had gone. He was as active and clumsy and playful as ever but the bull-like rushes had ceased. He was a different and more lovable cat.

The July sun expedited Charles's cure and convalescence, and soon the time came for the family to go away for the annual holiday by the sea. I was to join them later and Charles kept me company in London until I could go.

Our summer holidays in those days were very much a family affair. Except for Rupert the canary and the goldfish, who were boarded out, all the animals, even the white mice, accompanied us. Florence Nightingale, who never travelled without her cats – and she had many more than we had – would have approved. The cavalcade of baskets and other animal paraphernalia which passed in procession along railway station platforms must have been impressive, but I was usually too busy presiding over details of the journey to observe the interest we must have aroused in other travellers.

Minna and Peter were old hands at the game and knew what to expect when trunks and suit-cases were produced and opened. They viewed all the preparations with alarm. Peter barked his displeasure and Minna showed every sign of agitation, hiding her kittens and generally doing her best to be left behind. But I fancy it was no more than the nervousness of the bather who thinks the water will be too cold. Once in, all is well; and so it was with our animals. The journey over, they settled down to enjoy their holiday. I may say, in passing, that we never had the slightest fear of any of our cats straying from their holiday homes. They were kept in a quiet room while unpacking was done and after that they were allowed to make the usual thorough inspection of the new house. There may be some truth in the proverbial attachment of cats to houses but our cats at least were attached to us, wherever we were.

On this occasion Charles and I joined the family in the Isle of Wight, arriving late one Friday evening. We had taken a **furnished house** in Seagrove Bay, which was ideal for a family holiday, as sands and sea were directly in front of the house. It was a pleasant summer evening when Charles and I arrived, and after dinner and Charles's detailed examination of the house, a ceremony no cat neglects, I took him out on to the beach. There was a bright moon and we had the beach to ourselves. At Fowey the year before Charles had only once seen the sea at close quarters and I was curious to see if he remembered that somewhat alarming experience. Whether it was the effect of the moon, which is said to have an influence on cats, or the deserted beach or the quiet mood of the sea I do not know, but something had an immediately intoxicating effect on Charles. He leaped from my arms and raced all over the sands chasing his shadow, hiding behind rocks and pouncing out on me when I went after him. He ran into the creaming, phosphorescent surf and darted out again. He leapt into the air like an inspired ballet dancer, jumping rocks with the grace and agility of a steeplechaser and was not content until I joined him in a breathless game of hide and seek.

It was a memorable experience, which was never repeated. By day he ignored the sea with lofty dignity and refused to be tempted on to the beach. At night when all was quiet he made his way on to the sands and solemnly reconnoitred the rocks, seaweed and the pools of water, gazing Narcissus-like in their unruffled surface. But he would not play, and clearly preferred to be alone.

He spent most of his time that holiday basking in the

sun. One of his favourite places was a window sill on the first floor and it was while he was sunning himself there one day that he overbalanced and fell. By great good fortune there was a clump of thick bushes below and he landed right in the middle of them, to emerge none the worse for his fall.

Otherwise the holiday was uneventful and Charles seemed glad to return to Regent's Park and his familiar haunts. We remained there for the next four years, and except for occasional weekends away and one visit to America I was not separated from Charles. He became my constant companion. Minna accepted the position with equanimity. She had her kittens to think about and I imagine she thought of little else, for no sooner had one litter of kittens grown to the unmanageable age than another batch was on the way. She was a devoted and efficient mother and as time went on she seemed to have little interest in other matters, although she was still capable of a capricious affection.

Charles on the other hand became more and more devoted to me, and I confess I was not a little proud of his devotion. It was pleasant to find him waiting patiently on the stairs when I came home late; and however late it was he was nearly always there. Usually he greeted me with demonstrative affection but sometimes, if I were very late, he would pretend to be annoyed. On such occasions he would wait until I went upstairs, instead of scampering down to meet me in the hall, and when I bent down to stroke him he would dart out of my reach, just to put me in my place. But this affectation of indifference or disapproval never lasted long; a few minutes later and he would be purring at the top of his voice and thrusting his head hard against my legs until I picked him up and made a fuss of him.

He enjoyed petting but he also liked a rough-and-tumble, chasing me and being chased in turn, with no quarter given or asked for. But however ferociously he stabbed at me with his hind legs and outstretched claws, however fiercely his sharp teeth were poised over my hand, I knew there was nothing to fear from them: and I think he too knew that he would come to no harm at my hands.

As a full-grown cat he was just as inquisitive as when he was a kitten. Whenever I went with Shirley to the Zoo I brought back some novelty for his inspection, and I still remember with amusement his intense interest in tufts of camel hair – extracted from a camel, when the keepers were not looking, I am ashamed to say – porcupine quills, exotic feathers and such-like reminders of the strange fauna of the outside world. The strongly smelling camel's hair was his special delight and a nosegay of it tied to a piece of string would attract him for hours. And he would sniff with tireless interest at my coat when I came back after spending some time in my favourite place at the Zoo, the small cat house. The lingering odour of kinkajous and other creatures I had handled excited him queerly.

While we were at Regent's Park I acquired a pair of gerbils, a species of Egyptian sand rat. They were given to me by a friend who, I suspect, did not know what to do with them and correctly surmised that another strange animal or two could easily be accommodated in our domestic menagerie. They lived in a long cage which conveniently fitted on to the mantelpiece of my writing room. Charles, of course, showed the liveliest interest in these agile little creatures, and was fascinated when I allowed him to play with them. At first he thought there must be some catch in it, and refused to touch them. The gerbils, for their part, showed no sign of fear. When Charles saw me playing with them – and I let them out of their cage to run about the room – he decided to join in. If he showed any emotion it was perhaps a slight jealousy at my interest in these new pets.

They did not, alas, survive the winter. I learned too late that they cannot live at a low temperature, and they both died within a few days of the cold weather.

It surprised many people to hear that Charles had shown no aggressive attitude towards animals bearing such a close resemblance in human eyes to rats; but to Charles they probably looked, smelled and behaved very differently from ordinary rats. Not that he was ever an enthusiastic pursuer of either rats or mice. He would look on with polite interest while Minna and her kittens caught mice, and sometimes would himself pretend to watch a likely-looking hole. But he rarely bothered himself with mice and when he did I am sure it was only out of curiosity. When, some years later, we lived in the country and rats were to be found in abundance in the adjacent farm buildings Charles ignored them completely. He caught and disposed of a mouse or two, with the air of one who demonstrates that he knows how (this chiefly for the benefit of the other cats) but to the best of my knowledge he never caught a rat, or even tried to.

His interest in birds, apart from the fun to be had in his early days when Rupert's stand could be knocked over, was also perfunctory. The sentimentalist in me would like to record that he never caught a bird, but that would not be true. But it is true to say that he had no enthusiasm for killing birds. As he grew older he watched birds with mild interest but made no attempt to stalk them. He wore a collar which for many years had a bell attached, but I am sure this made no difference. Minna also had a collar and bell but soon learned how to prevent it from tinkling when she wormed her way across the garden in pursuit of a careless bird.

When Rupert the canary died from old age and rheumatism I presented my wife with two budgerigars. It was not safe to leave them outside a cage while Minna was about, but I do not think Charles would have harmed them. He liked to watch them, attracted no doubt by their brilliant plumage and flashing movements. When we moved to a new house an aviary was built in the garden, more budgerigars added, and Charles was able to lie in the sun and watch them to his heart's content.

In every way Charles became a gentle cat, as I have said, even to the extent of avoiding encounters with other cats. In spite of himself he sometimes became involved with other cats in the neighbourhood, but only in self-defence; and then, I regret to say, he escaped to safety as soon as he could.

Late one afternoon I heard a piercing din in the garden, and a long drawn-out howl which could only have come from Charles. I hurried out, just in time to chase away one of the most savage and disreputable cats I have ever seen. To my horror I then saw a good inch of Charles's tail on the ground beside him. It had been bitten off by the other cat. (This cat was a half-wild cat who had been roaming the neighbourhood, I heard later, attacking other cats and even dogs. He was eventually caught and disposed of by an animal welfare organization.) Poor Charles seemed stunned by what had happened, as well he might. I could not get through to Cartland on the telephone and in desperation mixed a strong disinfectant solution and put the end of Charles's tail in it for a minute or two. This amateur first-aid proved successful, as it turned out, and Charles was none the worse except for a shortened tail; but I do not recommend such treatment to others.

At another time something went wrong with one of Charles's forepaws and Bryan Cartland treated it. To prevent Charles from biting off the bandage, which he at once attempted, I made, on Cartland's instructions, a large cardboard collar. This fitted over Charles's head and being about twelve inches in diameter effectively prevented him from making contact between mouth and paws. Charles was furious at this affront to his dignity. To make matters worse everyone laughed at him; and indeed he was a comical sight.

But I did not laugh the next morning when Charles was missing. He disappeared for two days and it was only after many hours' frantic search that I found him cowering miserably in the area of a house a hundred yards away. I am sure he felt in some way disgraced, and there is little doubt in my mind that he ran away, or at any rate tried to hide until the humiliating contraption removed itself from his head. Luckily the bandage was still on his foot when I found him, although dirty, and when it was taken off the paw had almost healed. So all was well again.

Another episode was more amusing. We had acquired a wireless set with a loud speaker, then something of a novelty, and this toy was a source of interest, but only for a short time, to our inquisitive Siamese. After careful examination he obviously dismissed it as unworthy of further notice. But, long afterwards, when I made my first broadcast I asked my wife to be sure to have Charles in the room at the time. It was a talk on Siamese cats and I mentioned Charles by name. She assured me afterwards that when he heard my voice he was unmistakably puzzled and intrigued, and walked over to the loud speaker to try to get to the bottom of the mystery. I am sorry to have to record that he did not listen for more than a minute or so but went to sleep as though such realistic imitations were not good enough to deceive an intelligent cat.

When it amused him, however, Charles was very willing to be deceived. In the matter of stuffed toys for example. I bought in Birmingham the most realistic toy cat I have ever seen. In size and shape it was astonishingly life-like, and the fur looked and felt just like a cat's. I put it on the hearth-rug when Charles was not looking, and he was very much taken aback when he came into the room. But when he found, as he quickly did, that it was not a real cat, instead of turning away in disgust as I had expected, he began to play with it, obviously willing to keep up the pretence. He was, after that, always interested in toy animals and could easily be induced to play with them. I could never be sure, however, whether he played to amuse himself or me. 'When I play with my cat,' wrote Montaigne, 'who knows whether she diverts herself with me, or I with her?'

CHAPTER FOUR

In the summer of 1935 we moved to a house in St. John's Wood. Although near the heart of London St. John's Wood is in many ways agreeably rural. You can hear the birds sing in the daytime and at night the hooting of owls competes with the distant sound of motor traffic passing along the main roads. We had our share of trees, including an almond tree in the pleasant garden at the back of the house and an acacia tree in the small front garden, which my wife surveyed with the enthusiastic eye of the amateur gardener. She announced that she 'could make something of it' and in due course she did, although I dissuaded her from installing a goldfish pond in front of the house.

Charles, Minna and the other animals whose opinion counted were all in favour of the new house. There was no need to observe the amiable superstition – and superstition it is – of buttering the cats' paws. The new carpets met with their immediate approval and Charles lost no time in trying his claws on them.

After their first eager exploration indoors the cats began to reconnoitre the surrounding gardens and neighbourhood. I was rather anxious when Charles took to crossing the road, although there was not much traffic, because he was not used to a house which looked directly on to a road. At Regent's Park we lived in a terrace with a narrow private road separating the houses from a fair-sized strip of garden, beyond which our cats seldom ventured. Here in St. John's Wood cars and tradesmen's vans passed in larger numbers within a few yards of our front garden. However, I need not have worried, for Charles soon developed a traffic sense, although he seemed to take a mischievous delight in streaking across the road whenever he saw or heard a car approaching.

He was a friendly cat, and St. John's Wood is populated with animal lovers. In a very short time Charles had made friends with many of our neighbours. Indeed he knew many more people than we did. I discovered some time after we had been living there that he used to go regularly for meals to at least two other houses nearby. That explained his growing fastidiousness about food. He always had a good appetite except when he was ill and supplemented his main meal of the day – minced fresh meat – with various delicacies elsewhere. As there was always plenty to eat at home I am sure it was sociability and not greed which accounted for his frequent absences.

Where food was concerned Charles, like all cats, was an incorrigible thief. I have never been able to under-stand why intelligent human beings expect a cat to conform to their notions of morality and to refrain from taking food within his reach. A cat does not profess to be obedient. To him food is food wherever he finds it, and it would be manifestly absurd to neglect his oppor-tunities. What has man's code to do with him? As for people who try to cure a cat of stealing by punishment, I have no patience with them. It is simply cruel.

The cat's instincts in this connexion are fundamen-tal. It is easy to teach a cat to be clean because he is by nature clean. But it is virtually impossible, in my exper-ience, to teach a cat to ignore food. There is no sense of guilt or shame in a cat caught in the act of stealing. Chase him away and he recognizes your dis-pleasure; but to him you are being wholly unreasonable.

That is all very well, I can imagine outraged house-wives and cooks exclaiming, but we can't have cats helping themselves to the contents of our larders. To which I can only say, do not keep a cat if you expect him to behave like a dog or a human being, who is temperamentally capable of obedience. The only rem-edy is to keep things out of his reach.

Nor can it be argued that a well-fed cat should be content with what is given to him. The cat has a dis-criminating appetite. He would rather steal a lobster at the risk of having a saucepan lid thrown at him than fill his belly with bread and milk from his own dish. In later years Charles would always help himself to butter if he got the chance, ignoring the margarine next to it

47

on the war-time table. He often refused unappetizing food, obviously in the hope that he would be able, if pleading failed, to lay his paws by skill or cunning on the more tempting food he knew was in reserve.

On one occasion he disgraced us by stealing a cold roast chicken from the house opposite. This house had been taken by the composer Roger Quilter, and Charles, having no respect for reputations, climbed through an open window and proudly carried his prize across the road. I caught him in the act, retrieved the chicken and went to make my apologies. Mr. Quilter had not yet arrived to take possession of the house but his manservant and wife were very nice about it and said that Charles was welcome. From that time on Charles made himself at home across the way. Roger Quilter himself told me a few years later of Charles's frequent visits. Once he interrupted a party. Charles was heard uttering his loud plaintive cry outside the drawing-room and insisted on his friend Mr. Quilter opening the door and letting him in.

When disinclined for visiting Charles spent much of his time sitting in state on the six-foot pillar overlooking the pavement in front of our house, accepting with condescension the admiration of friendly passers-by. I used to watch him from the window of my room on the first floor, highly amused at the airs and graces he gave himself. He liked admiration and friendly advances almost as much as he liked the warm sun, and on fine days there was plenty of both to be had.

The only fly in the ointment was a sinister orange-and-white tom-cat who lived nearby – we never discovered exactly where. He was the sort of disreputable tom who may have had no regular habitation. As cats go he was no beauty, to human eyes at any rate; torn-eared, dirty, proprietorial, virile and aggressive. Minna Minna Mowbray, of course, adored him. She had a weakness for rough and unbeautiful tom-cats and I suspect he was the father of many of her St. John's Wood kittens. Charles hated this tom and would run away at the sight of him; and I, who have never pretended to like all cats, also hated him and to make up for Charles's timidity scared him away whenever I could. But that made no difference. Old orange-and-white strutted over to our house whenever he felt like it, and Charles wisely avoided him as much as possible.

If he kept out of the way of strange cats Charles was the most sociable creature with human beings. At cock-tail parties he would mix freely with our guests, accepting homage and submitting with a good grace to being handled by strangers. It has often been remarked that cats readily approach people who have no conspicuous love of cats, even those who actively dislike them, but I do not think, as some do, that this is a perverse trait in the cat's character. It seems to me more likely that cats, like most animals, often fight shy of the outstretched hands and beckoning gestures of strangers, preferring to go to people who show no inclination to stroke them or pick them up. Although Charles could be sturdily independent when he chose he was nearly always friendlier than most cats I have known.

At dinner I encouraged him – and to this day my wife has not forgiven me – to sit on the table by my side. There he would remain until the sweet course was served, when his interest in the proceedings ceased. The *pièce de résistance* from his point of view was the fish or the main course, during which it was his privilege to be fed titbits. I fear some of our guests shared Edna's disapproval but those who were ardent cat-lovers approved, and to his credit it must be said that Charles comported himself with dignity.

Charles always knew beforehand what was for dinner. While I was dressing I had no need to ask what we were going to have. If the menu included roast pheasant, grouse or partridge, a barrage of ecstatic cries heralded the good news as the delicious smell reached his sensitive nose from the kitchen below. If it were merely plain roast chicken or grilled sole he gave utterance to less enthusiastic but nevertheless well-sustained reminders of his existence. For ordinary roast meat there was non-committal silence. He had well-defined preferences. Asparagus was one of his favourite dishes and he would surprise us by eating with relish such things as cheese, olives and beetroot. But when his olfactory nerve detected game he was in a seventh heaven and until dinner was served he would give me no peace, rubbing himself continuously against my legs and in the process covering my trousers with his white hairs.

The best authorities on the upbringing of cats will tell you that they should have regular meals and not be fed at odd times. For me and my cats that has always been a counsel of perfection. I have never been able to resist their appeals, vocal or silent, for a small share of the good things on my plate; and I do not really think they have been any the worse for this indulgence. One of the admirable characteristics of the adult cat is that he knows when he has had enough to eat, so there is no danger of over-feeding him. Although our cats have always had regular meals they seem to take a special pleasure in the tasty morsels they can coax out of us. It is to them clearly a privilege. On such occasions Minna and Charles would bestow on my wife's crestfallen dog a look of insufferable superiority; for my wife is stronger-minded than I, and holds the view that dogs should not be fed at table.

As he grew older and wiser Charles would turn up his nose at plain cold meat if he knew there was rabbit or poultry in the larder. It was no use anyone trying to pretend that cold meat was all there was. He knew better; and I at least always quailed under his disbelieving stare. When his food was to his liking he would eat it unhurriedly but in large gulps. I could always tell by the length of the pause between mouthfuls his degree of appreciation. Sometimes he registered dissatisfaction in the manner common to all cats; superciliously examining the food set in front of him, or turning it over with a disdainful paw. These preliminaries would be presently followed by a reproachful look from his blue eyes, and perhaps an offended squeak. If I did not respond he would turn his back on the offending dish and move slowly away, his whole body one eloquent rebuke.

I remember one day playing a trick on him. He had been given something uninteresting – I think it was cold fish – but rightly suspected that the remains of yesterday's pheasant was in the larder. When he put on his usual act, silently grumbling and touching the fish as though it would poison him if he ate it, I pretended not to notice and quickly went out of the room. Tiptoeing back, I peered through the crack in the half-closed door, to see Charles wolfing the fish as though he had never tasted or wanted anything better.

Our years in Acacia Road were undoubtedly among the happiest of Charles's life. It was a well ordered world and Charles must have felt as secure as our grandparents did in the settled and spacious days of Queen Victoria. The only innovations were other animals and Charles did not mind them. His place was assured.

We had two new pets before leaving Regent's Park: Edna now owned a fat Cairn terrier called Bunty, and Shirely had been given a rabbit. Bunty had only two interests in life – food and Edna. Peter the Rabbit, a Blue Beveren, was the most extraordinary rabbit I have ever known or heard of. He chased cats and dogs, all of whom were afraid of him. As he grew older he became more and more aggressive. Even Minna gave him a wide berth. Charles, I noticed promptly disappeared whenever Peter was allowed to run loose on the lawn, unless he were on my lap, where he presumably felt safe.

We also had an aquarium. This occupied a recess in the wall of the drawing-room and was filled with small tropical fish. This intrigued Charles and I can easily understand how the bubbling water and the brightly coloured, darting creatures fascinated him. They were however out of his reach; the goldfish in the nursery bowl was more tempting game, although his insinuating paw never did any harm. In fact the goldfish lived to a remarkable old age.

There were other attractions inside the house. The baby grand was much to Charles's liking. It was easier to negotiate than the old upright piano of our Regent's Park days, and there was plenty of room on top. Sometimes Charles would interrupt my playing by an unexpected jump on to the keys, and from there to the top, where he would sit and pretend he had only gone to wash himself at leisure. But I have known him go to sleep on top of the piano. Much as I loved him I deplored the marks of his claws when he made a more clumsy jump than usual or missed his footing, as he often did, on the slippery curved surface of the keyboard lid. But it was no use scolding Charles. He seemed to know that my heart was not in it, for he would only stare or blink at me as if I were being quite unreasonable. And if I raised my voice he would feign panic and run away, only to return a few minutes later as though nothing had happened.

He was, I think fond of me. But although he was my cat, following me about – and like most Siamese he followed like a dog – preferring my knee to any other, even sleeping most nights, especially during cold weather, on my bed, I cannot say that I had any exclusive right to his affection. He enjoyed his life wherever he was, and apportioned his good will among his many friends of the neighbourhood.

Apart from Peter the Rabbit and the orange-and-white tom he extended his good will to other animals. Most of Minna's kittens were given to our friends but Shirley was now old enough to have a cat of her own and she chose a long-haired tabby kitten for herself. This kitten, who looked like a cat drawn by Foujita, and would have been a real beauty had it not been for her plebeian little brown nose, was christened Priscilla Purr, a name destined inevitably to be abbreviated to Rissa. She was an independent little thing with amber eyes, and was mute like her mother. Shirley adored her. A long friendship between Charles and Rissa began in Acacia Road – but I shall have more to tell presently of Rissa.

There was another exception to Charles's tolerant attitude towards animals. My sister-in-law who lived in Dorset had a large family of cats, partly descended from our own cat family, and there was one exquisitely pretty cat whom I so greatly admired whenever I went to stay there that she very kindly offered her to me. Easter, as she was called, was a young silvery-grey cat with a lustrous coat and a most amiable disposition. She will always have the distinction of being the only cat I have ever coveted: and it is, by the way, a curious thing that we rarely covet other people's pets although we may often break the tenth commandment in all other respects.

Charles was now in such a good mood that I antici-pated no objection on his part to the addition of Easter to our collection of household pets, but to my surprise he took a fierce and instant dislike to her. Perhaps it was because I made the mistake of installing her in my own room when she arrived. That room Charles rightly regarded as his domain; and I only made matters worse when I excluded him by shutting the door and leaving him on the outside. He refused to go away but crouched outside, sniffing under the crack of the closed door and growling his anger. When he caught sight of Easter he spat resentfully and would, I believe, have attacked her. So a few days later, when it was plain he was not going to relent, I had to send poor Easter back to Dorset.

After her departure he bore no malice. He sniffed suspiciously at the carpet in my room but that was the only sign of his disapproval, and he soon resumed his comfortable routine.

We were still living near the Zoo and whenever I went there I remembered to bring back something of interest for Charles. The pungent camel's hair never failed to excite his eager interest. Other souvenirs he sniffed at and sometimes played with according to his mood and, I presume, their varying olfactory attraction. He must have been vastly puzzled by my mysterious outings at the week-end, when if I did not come back with bits of fur or feathers in a paper bag I smelt strangely myself. One Sunday I went to see Pickles the one-year-old bear, who vigorously licked my hands. Charles could not make out what I had been up to. He sniffed intently at my hands and raised his voice in bewilderment.

My favourite in the Zoo at that time was Billy the wart hog, at the sight of whom most casual visitors shuddered. Billy was however the most enchanting creature when you knew him. The best way to get to know him, incidentally, was to give him chocolate, and many of my pennies went into the slot machine near his cage. I would dearly have liked to take Charles to the Zoo and introduce him to my other animal friends but, perhaps fortunately, it was against the rules. Charles would have had the fright of his life; although the two Siamese cats which belonged to a keeper in the Lion House seemed quite indifferent to the strange medley of smells and noises around them.

At week-ends, when I was at home, I brushed and combed Charles regularly, not because he needed it but because he liked it. I had bought him a comb and a brush, with bristles as tough as wire. These were kept in a paper bag in my desk, and I had only to produce the bag for Charles to follow me with every appearance of delight. He liked to be brushed and combed vigorously and I could do what I pleased with him; turning him on his back, standing him on his hind legs, anything so long as I went on using the brush and comb. He had a thick coat and at certain times of the year large quantities of fur came off in the process. None of my cats ever enjoyed being barbered so much as Charles. His purring was one continuous roll of muffled drums.

By domestic tradition I had a room of my own which served both as a dressing-room and a room in which to work. Charles had the freedom of this room and usually went to sleep on my desk when the sun shone on it. The scratching of a pen on paper always attracted him and he got into the habit of interrupting my work. But it is hardly fair to describe as interruptions his gentle intrusions. When I was writing or reading he used to jump on the desk and after one or two half-hearted attempts to persuade me to stop what I was doing and attend to him, he would lie down and go to sleep, sometimes inconveniently sprawled across the papers I was using. I liked to have him with me, for he always knew when I wanted him to be quiet; and there is something very tranquil and soothing about a sleeping cat. No human being can extinguish his presence as a cat does. He soon learned the art of going to sleep on my knee when I was sitting in an armchair reading a manuscript and often allowed me to use him as a book rest.

And how pleased he was if I tired of reading and woke him up for a game! Hide and seek, chasing a ball of paper which he delighted in retrieving, or just a rough and tumble – anything for a game. I taught him not to mind when I picked him up and coiled him over my head like a living bearskin: he would stay there unprotestingly until I lifted him down again. He had his games too, and seemed to reserve a special liveliness for the hour before bed-time. He always liked to be with me when I undressed, and still hid himself when I took off shoes and socks so that he could make a lightning pounce on my bare feet before I had time to get them into slippers. Even if my feet were protected there was still fun to be had with my legs, at which he would take a playful little bite when he got the chance, just as a horse or goat will affectionately nibble someone they know. We talked together the whole time: no doubt the servants thought it very odd. The family of course were quite used to the absurd conversations that went on inside my dressing-room and took no notice.

The importance of human legs in the cat's world is often over-looked. As I have said earlier, one of Charles's endearing habits was to rub his head vigorously against my legs. It was as though he were saying, 'Why do you have to wear those silly trousers? I can't get *at* you.' Strange legs were different, of course. Some people's legs are clumsy, even unkind: they have to be watched carefully. Long skirts are a menace to a sensitive cat: women cannot always be counted on to avoid brushing into a cat as they go by. Children's legs are dangerously active and unreliable. Yes, a cat must consider human legs very important. They are for most of the time the nearest part of those queerly erect human bodies, and one must always be ready to jump out of the way. And, as for the few people one knows and loves, how else can a cat remind an upright human being of his existence, of his desire to be noticed and petted? It's no use talking to them, I can imagine a cat saying to himself, they are so stupid; they think you're hungry or want to be let out, or have a pain.

With me at all events Charles seemed to know he would not be misunderstood. When he stroked his back against my leg and turned round to do it on the other side he knew I would understand, and bend down to caress him or pick him up. He loved to be picked up and held like a baby. He was as much at ease on my shoulder as on the ground and purred his continuous pleasure. Besides all these exhibitions of his affection he had one habit which in my experience of cats is unique. As soon as I took off my shoes he would transfer his attention to them, rubbing his head against each shoe in turn, and even pushing the shoe along the ground in his pleasure.

From my dressing-room he would follow me to my bed, which he regarded as partly his property. In cold weather he liked to sleep under the eiderdown. He had a decided preference for the middle of the bed and seemed not to mind my feet. If he were still in a playful mood he amused himself by trying to bite, or rather pretending to bite, my feet through the blankets. He bore no malice if I accidentally kicked him aside in the night, but that was no easy matter, for he was a heavy cat. *J'y suis, j'y reste* was his motto, and no matter how much I disturbed him, even to the point of pushing him off the bed altogether, back he would come and settle down again to sleep.

He did not sleep regularly on my bed, sometimes preferring his open basket or a chair in one of the other rooms. He seldom went out at night, although he had a mischievous habit of asking to be let out an hour or so before bed-time. This was usually in the summer, and on warm nights he would take a delight in staying out until I had undressed. He knew perfectly well that I would come down in my dressing-gown, open the door and clap my hands – the recognized signal for calling him in. Many a time – usually when the moon was full and went to his head – he pretended not to hear, and only when I had lost patience and had nearly roused the whole neighbourhood clapping my hands and shouting at him would he dash into the house; usually from a place of concealment a few yards away, where he had been laughing to himself all the time.

CHAPTER FIVE

During the four years we lived in St. John's Wood I was never away from home for more than a few days, except for holidays and another visit to New York in the early part of 1939. Charles watched my preparations for departure with even more than his customary gloom, no doubt observing that it was not the time of year for the family holiday. The cabin trunk, too, was filled, not with summer clothes belonging to the family but with my things only. He was so disconsolate – or maybe disgusted – that when the time came to say good-bye he hid under my bed and would not come out.

I was back within a month – and Charles took no notice of me. He was still sulking. It was the only time in his life that he ever sulked. But he relented within a few hours, in fact as soon as we were alone together; and I began to wonder whether his attitude was due to

the presence of others. One thing I can say with convic-
tion. He was always a different cat in public, even in
the family circle. When we were alone together he
played more boisterously and was more lavish with his
affection. With anyone else about he kept up a pretence
of dignity. Even so he was much more responsive than
any other cat I have known. He would come when he
was called; jump on my knee at the slightest invitation
and often without it; play the games I have described;
and follow me devotedly. But an air of restraint marked
all his attentions in public.

To anyone but a cat-lover this may seem merely fanciful; and I am not unaware of the danger which besets
all lovers of animals when they contemplate the indi-
viduality of their pets. It is easy to exaggerate their
flattering attentions, and almost as easy to imagine
things that have no reality. But I think it is part of the
cat's peculiar charm that he so often discards his natural reticence when he is alone with the human being
who is to him most important. At any rate I have no
hesitation in saying that Charles reserved for our
strictly private intercourse the most lovable traits in his
character. With this knowledge in my mind it was
amusing to observe his consistently affectionate behaviour in private and his pretence of dignity and independence in public – when he happened to remember.

While we were living in St. John's Wood Charles
received an invitation to become the vice-president of a
society formed under the title 'The Honourable Company of Cats' to raise funds for sick animal dispensaries
in London districts; and I accepted on his behalf. Mlle

Alicia Markova's black cat Tinker was president, and the patrons included the Mansion House cat, Richard Whittington, owned by the daughter of the then Lord Mayor, Miss Ennis Twyford; the Marquis of Casa Maury's cat, Marina; Mr. X, Cavalier and Parker, Beverley Nichols's three cats; Val Gielgud's Hugo; and the Manchester Deanery cat, Binky Bill, owned by Miss Sheila Williams. On the committee were over a score of cats famous in their own right or by virtue of their owners' celebrity: among them Yvonne Arnaud's Minerva, Nathaniel Gubbins's Sally (probably the best-known cat in all England), Collie Knox's Peter, Marie Lohr's Coronation Corrie, and Max Saltmarsh's noble cat Victoria, who had honoured me with her personal friendship.

Charles accepted his public position with dignity. He posed for press photographers and generally behaved as if he knew what all the fuss was about. I have always regretted that the owners of all the celebrated cats who held official positions did not bring their pets with them to the Mansion House for the inaugural luncheon, for I am sure Charles would have enjoyed his rôle of vice-president on that delectable occasion. But perhaps it was just as well.

However, a few months later, when I was in a nursing home for a short time, Charles, by kind permission of the matron, was allowed to come to tea. On that occasion he behaved as though he were quite accustomed to visiting nursing homes, and sat on my bed with unruffled calm. He was a very sociable cat and was on his best behaviour with the nurses who, I suspect, were secretly scandalized by this breach of nursing home decorum.

He was also a very conversational cat, especially when we were alone together. He understood every inflection of my voice; and I learned to know the meaning of at least some of his many cries. To a stranger and even, I believe, to other people who knew him well, his plaintive voice must have sounded the same note whenever he used it. But anyone who has lived close to a Siamese cat knows that he has a wide range of expression. I could always distinguish between Charles's cry for a door to be opened, his demands for food, his requests for notice to be taken of him.

He had his own peculiar and distinguishable utterances for various occasions: as for instance when he had made use of his tray and wanted to be sure that it would be made ready for him again. He could be assertive without being clamorous: he could talk softly and as he grew older he often did. He could even make himself understood silently when he chose.

Sometimes in the night he would be distressed – could it have been bad dreams? – and would awake me with a strident and insistent clamour, and that was something not to be borne patiently, for I defy anyone to sleep through a Siamese fortissimo. But although as I came to the surface from the depths of sleep I momentarily lost patience even with Charles, I could not be truly angry with him.

He liked to have his own way, and he had many different ways of getting it. There were times when his voice was pure honey, and the touch of his paw so gentle that it could scarcely be felt. If he sensed that I had other things on my mind he would approach me cautiously, so that I was almost unaware of his slow, ingratiating progress. When I petted one of the other cats he gave me a basilisk stare until I remembered my obligations and transferred my affection to him. If I took no notice of him, preferring to sit at the piano, he jumped past me and sat serenely on a level with my head as if he were taking part in the entertainment. He used me increasingly as a pillow, lying asleep on my knee and sometimes dreaming perhaps of unfought battles, his delicately formed mouth slightly open, revealing his white teeth bared in a harmless snarl, his long whiskers bristling. Sometimes he persuaded me to open a drawer for him, so that he could climb into it and settle down with deep satisfaction for a sleep.

Now that he was staid and middle-aged I was more fond of him than ever. My affection for him was intensified by the anxiety I felt for the future; for this was 1939, and who could tell what was going to happen? We had often discussed tentative plans in the event of war breaking out. I had already made up my mind that I would rejoin the army if the War Office would have me, and that raised the question of disposing of my family. It was finally settled that if war came they would leave London and live for the time being in the country and that the animals should go with them.

When war did come it was too late to take Minna. She was now old and ailing; and it would have been cruel to inflict on her the strain of a war-time journey in the hope that she could be happily transplanted to another home. It was a difficult decision to make, but I finally decided that she should, in the gentle phrase which children use, be put to sleep. It was ironical that I should have to put down one of the best-loved of all my cats.

The budgerigars could not be transported and they too had to be destroyed. Charles, Rissa (now grown into a very personable young lady) and Peter the Rabbit went to Sussex with us. There had been some doubt about Peter, for he too was getting old; but Shirley tearfully insisted that he should be spared. He lived only a few months longer, during which his temper became even more uncertain. In the end it was not safe to go near him unless armed with a stick or golf club, for he took to biting ankles without provocation. He was indeed a rabbit of great valour.

Charles viewed the prospect of country life with obvious misgivings. This was the time of year when his familiar warm places and cosy corners assumed a daily increasing importance, and to judge by his dejected appearance he did not relish the change of scene. For a few weeks our temporary home was a house with a large and lovely garden, but for poor Charles the garden was alive with menace. The gardener's cat had his home there, and the gardener's cat was savage. He was so wild that none of us could go near him. Naturally enough he resented Charles's intrusion in his territory and lay in wait for him, and one day the inevitable clash occurred. As usual Charles came off second best, although it was no disgrace to be bowled over by such a fierce and hardened opponent. In the battle one of

Charles's ears suffered injury. It filled out and I had to take him to the nearest veterinary surgeon. At the first opportunity I took him back to London, where I left him for a day or two with his old friend Bryan Cartland. He emerged with the equivalent of a boxer's cauliflower ear, which gave him an odd appearance: one ear erect and the other crumpled. But otherwise he seemed none the worse for his misadventure, and although unkind people laughed or stared he was dearer to me than ever.

More trials were in store for Charles that winter. We moved to Mayfield in Sussex and lived there for several months. The winter of 1939 – 1940 was bitterly cold and it was impossible to keep warm in the house. Outside, for it was a farmhouse, there were cows, and Charles had never had anything to do with cows. He disliked them on sight. In a field on the other side of the house there was a horse, and Charles would have nothing to do with him either. It was no consolation to my poor shivering Charles that Shirley had realized a long-cherished ambition and was actually living on a farm. We did not find out until long after that she used to sleep with an alarm clock under her pillow so that she could creep out in the snow and darkness to help the farmer with his cows.

Another of her ambitions now realized was to keep hens. Charles did not object to hens and after he had inspected them at close quarters he evidently came to the conclusion that they were not worth bothering about. The indifference of cats to hens is curious. To cats there seems nothing bird-like about hens, and I doubt if they see any connexion between the foolish clumsy birds and the succulent roast chickens which appear on the table.

As I belonged to the Army Officers Emergency Reserve I expected to be recalled to the army any day; and in the meantime I went to and fro between Sussex and London, living alone in the house at St. John's Wood and joining the family at week-ends. To alleviate my loneliness, and also because Charles seemed miserable at Mayfield, I used to take him with me to London. He had always shown a lively interest in cars and soon adapted himself to the routine of our journeys. He always stepped cheerfully into his basket and as a rule went comfortably to sleep. Sometimes he liked to make himself heard and would keep up a flow of plaintive conversation throughout the journey. He was always glad to return to his old haunts in St. John's Wood and he had so many friends there that I had no anxiety about leaving him alone during the day.

When spring came he showed more interest in his surroundings at Mayfield, although he continued to give a wide berth to the farm animals. There was a winding, neglected stream near the house which yielded small trout, and Charles discovered that he liked freshly caught trout. I spent many hours alone fishing in the stream and listening to the distant rumble of gunfire as the Battle of France worked up to its tragic climax.

We left Mayfield in the early summer to live in Kent; but we were there only a short time. My long-awaited medical board was followed a few weeks later by notification that I had been posted to a battalion of the Queen's Own Royal West Kent Regiment. I returned to London at once, and the family followed. Charles no doubt rejoiced to see us all back, and probably wondered why we had ever committed the folly of leaving London at all. But he soon had cause for other anxiety, for he could tell by the family atmosphere that more changes were imminent.

His sorrowful expression when he saw me in uniform, hurriedly packing for departure, remains in my memory. My heart was heavy too, for the future was highly uncertain, and I might never see him again. I said good-bye sadly: it is one of the tragedies of our friendships with animals that we cannot reassure them with gay and cheerful promises of an early reunion. To them separation is a dreadful thing, which cannot be explained.

Charles had the consolation of his familiar friends and surroundings, I reminded myself, and would soon get used to my absence. He would accept that as he had learned to accept other happenings beyond his control or understanding. For me a new and exacting life had begun and I had no time for melancholy reflection. I did not know then that the war was destined to bring us closer together.

In August 1940 the Germans launched their first air raids on London. In addition to anxiety for my family I was greatly worried about Charles. Bombs and guns were not only instruments of potential destruction; they were to be dreaded for their appalling noise alone, and I could not bear to think of Charles and Rissa cowering in terror during raids. I heard with relief from my wife that Bryan Cartland had agreed to look after them at his home in the country. And so the cats left the house in St. John's Wood, never to see it again, for it was badly damaged in a later raid. Before their departure could be arranged however they endured some frightening experiences. Edna's dog Bunty had died while we were at Mayfield, and I think she was now almost glad, for Bunty dreaded noise.

My battalion was temporarily stationed near a town in Worcestershire and although raids were made from time to time on the Midlands we escaped the attentions of enemy aircraft. It was a bewildering and by no means pleasant thought that having joined the army I should be in peaceful surroundings while my family and many of my civilian friends had to endure bombing. I was however so preoccupied with training that there was little time for disagreeable thoughts of this kind, which would have been useless in any case. The army claimed all my time.

Yet I was not too busy to notice the pretty little black kitten who had attached himself to the officers' mess and was being thoroughly spoiled by everyone, from the colonel downwards. This kitten lived on the fat of the land and was a great favourite, especially with the mess staff.

In October the battalion was given an operational rôle – a distinction for a battalion which had been formed only a few months earlier – and, to use one of the army's favourite verbs, we proceeded to the south coast, at that stage of the war part of Britain's front line.

CHAPTER SIX

Although I had been in the army for only three months my former comfortable existence seemed already to belong to a distant past. We were working under severe pressure, but military life had one compensation. There was no time for meditation. We were living in a vulnerable present which excluded all thought of the past and very nearly all contemplation of the future. The arrival of more automatic weapons and ammunition, intensive training and preparations against the invasion which then seemed imminent – such matters obliged us to live almost entirely for day to day responsibilities.

But, as the days went swiftly past, and every day saw an improvement in our hastily improvised defences, we began to breathe more easily. There was time to play with the perky little kitten which had been given to one of my brother officers by a lady in Worcestershire who thought, quite rightly, that no infantry company was complete without a mascot. This kitten had settled down happily in the company officers' mess. At the time the battalion was responsible for many miles of the coast and the rifle companies each had separate headquarters. The black kitten I have already mentioned, now growing into a sleek and satisfied cat, had accompanied battalion headquarters and had become a great favourite with the colonel.

Our kitten, also black, with bright intelligent eyes and an inexhaustibly playful spirit, had been christened Victor by Bernard Russell, who in those early days commanded a platoon in my company. Having been presented with the kitten, he considered it right and proper that he should name it. But that did not suit me. Victor seemed to me a silly name for such a playful kitten and, exercising my *droit de seigneur* both as company commander and as one with some experience of cats, I announced that in future Victor would be called Ticky-Wee. Bernard, who had that independence of spirit which went so well with his reddish hair, vociferously insisted that Victor should remain Victor. Gradually, however everyone began calling Victor by his new name, and even Bernard had to laugh when I caught him addressing his Victor as Ticky-Wee. So Ticky-Wee he was.

It was no doubt the propinquity of Ticky-Wee and the colonel's invariable mention of *his* cat whenever he visited our company headquarters that started my train of thought. I knew Charles was safe and happy with his friend Bryan Cartland, but after all he was my cat.

Now that the first anxious days of my new army life had passed, why, I thought, should I not have Charles with me?

In the last war I had two cats on active service. One, Scissors by name, was a bonny little black and white cat who appeared from nowhere when I was in the line near Arras. I adopted him gratefully, and he stayed with my machine gun section until we moved to another part of the line. He was last seen trotting across No-Man's-Land towards the German trenches. It was a quiet sector at the time, and I can only hope that the Bavarians across the way treated him kindly. My other cat was also a stray, and a most intelligent cat. She learned to squeeze condensed milk out of a punctured tin, a habit which made her unpopular when we ran short of milk for tea. Lillywhite was however an independent cat, and I am ashamed to say she eventually deserted me for the sergeants' mess.

Charles however was the best loved of all my cats and I was tremendously excited at the possibility of having him with me. It was of course necessary to ask the colonel's permission. Fortunately the colonel, although a strict disciplinarian, liked cats: and he had heard about Charles on many occasions. I do not think he realized how important it was to me, but he gave his permission readily. How I rejoiced!

Arrangements were speedily made and Charles and Rissa were brought from the country to London, and from there sent by train to Dorset. My family had left London not long before and had found a furnished cottage some miles in the rear of the battalion area. Like most of the battalions formed since Dunkirk we were still short of transport and I had pressed into military service the ancient car I had bought on the outbreak of war. This enabled me to meet the train which brought the cats on their southbound journey. The station was near the cottage where my family were living and as soon as I had handed over Rissa to Shirley, who was as delighted to see her again as I was to see Charles, I headed the car for the coast to introduce Charles to his new quarters.

The long journey must have been uncomfortable for him, for he was not used to the indignity of the guard's van, and for some days after his arrival he was not at all himself. He greeted me affectionately but his lack of appetite and his ruffled coat were signs of his *malaise*. The weather which had turned cold increased his discomfort and for several days he sat stiffly by the fire, ignoring all advances and taking no interest in his new surroundings.

My billet was at the officers' mess near company headquarters and from my bedroom I had a good view of the sea about a hundred yards away. In summer it would have been ideal but even in November it was a pleasant place to live in. Charles gradually shook off his indisposition, snubbed the playful advances of Ticky-Wee, and made the best of a bad job by occupying the warmest corners during the day and educating the mess staff, already his devoted admirers, up to his gastric standards.

It must have been a strange new world for Charles. Used as he was to a household presided over by women, the tramp of heavy army boots and the loud voices of an exclusively male community were not at all agreeable. He was now in his eleventh year and, like Arnold Bennett, he had discovered the pleasures of routine in middle age. All cats are conservative, disliking change more and more as they grow older; and Charles was a most conservative cat. He must have sadly missed his former placid life, with its domestic routine: the regular visits of tradesmen at the back door, the voices of women and children, the company of his great friend Rissa, and all the familiar sights and smells and noises of his own neighbourhood. Whenever he had been away from home before there had been at least something of his own background with him, and even during his stay with the Cartlands he had had Rissa for company and the background of a well run household.

Here on the south coast everything was different. Even I, his sole link with the old happy days, was a different person, wearing strange uniform and heavy boots, and behaving in an unaccountably odd fashion. Instead of leaving and returning home at regular hours I was in and out at all times of the day and night. I remember how pathetically he stared at me when I got out of bed in the middle of the night and put on my equipment to go round the defence posts. The strange voices, too, which interrupted the peace of the night, with news of messages just received; the sound of army trucks and motor bicycles driving up at all hours; the uncarpeted floors; the sounds of loud laughter and men singing just before Lights Out; the general atmosphere and bustle of military activity: all this must have bewildered my poor Charles.

But in spite of their desire to cling to familiar things cats will adapt themselves to a new life, and so it was with Charles. There were compensations. Army food was good and plentiful; there were sunny days even in November; and he had many admirers. He soon became used to the strange, outlandish speech of the officers' servants who comprised the mess staff and they, like all British soldiers, had a staunch liking for animals. Before long he had supplanted Ticky-Wee in their affections.

The colonel came over to see him and, I fancy, was not at first impressed. Perhaps I had over-sung his praises; perhaps it was because Charles was not looking his best on that day, which was wet and cold. In consequence he sat crouching unsociably by the meagre fire, staring morosely into space. I never knew a cat who could look so forlorn and dejected when he chose. However, the colonel, who was always polite on non-military subjects, greeted him amiably and went off, as I heard later, to talk about my 'thousand pound cat with one ear' in the battalion mess. The colonel had a sense of humour.

The officers in my company, who had more opportunity of seeing Charles, were on the whole admiring and friendly. Privately they no doubt thought that Charles was an odd creature with his strange colouring and strident voice, but they soon came to know that he was a cat of remarkable character. Leonard Olney, one of the platoon commanders, was one of his earliest and most steadfast admirers. Leonard was a great lover of animals and stoutly defended Charles when irresponsible criticisms were made – with the object, as I well knew, of pulling my leg in approved military fashion.

But of all Charles's friends in the battalion my batman Galea was the most faithful. Galea, a Maltese, had been my servant since the battalion's earliest days, and was used to the peculiarities of my behaviour. To Galea there was nothing surprising in my sending for my favourite cat, even a one-eared Siamese. Charles captured his affection at once. It was fortunate for Charles that I had Galea as a batman, for Galea had a genius, invaluable in an officer's servant, for creating comfort out of chaos, and for finding (scrounging is the army word) useful additions to the amenities of military life. Did Charles like fish? Fish was obtained. Tender lean steak? A clean blanket? Fresh milk? More coal on the fire? Roast chicken? (This was in 1940!) All were produced in miraculously short time. Lest it be thought that Galea purloined government property I hasten to make it clear that a hotel and civilian households functioned near our headquarters. I have good reason to suspect that Galea's disarming smile and gentle Maltese accent softened many a susceptible feminine heart in a good cause.

As he settled down Charles became more and more proprietorial, as was his custom. The mess and my bedroom were his headquarters but he seemed to realize that by virtue of being my cat he had the right to go where he pleased in the company area. The men, most of whom had never seen or heard of a Siamese cat before, soon became accustomed to the sight of Charles sunning himself outside the officers' mess whenever the weather was encouraging. But as the days became shorter and the weather more uninviting Charles preferred to stay indoors.

The company sergeant-major, who had definite ideas on most subjects, including animals, obviously did not quite know what to make of Charles. There was clearly a conflict in his mind. On the one hand Charles was the company commander's cat and as such entitled to a measure of respect; at the same time the C.S.M. did not approve of innovations, and a Siamese cat was something new. And, by all appearances, unmilitary. The sergeant-major compromised with his conscience by announcing firmly that he was a dog-lover.

When the company moved to another sector of the coast Charles took up residence at company headquarters. Our bedroom was directly above the company office and as the rest of the house was cold Charles spent most of his time in the company office, where there was a large and hospitable fire. Outside in the snow Ticky-Wee climbed on the sentry's shoulder, putting military dignity in peril, but Charles was too old for such kittenish amusements. He preferred the fire indoors.

It so happened that the sergeant-major's table and chair were nearest to the fire, and Charles made no bones about occupying one or the other, according to the degree of heat spreading from the fire and the all-important matter of draughts. It did not concern

Charles in the least whether or not the sergeant-major wanted to sit in his chair or put his elbows on the table. If the chair was already occupied when Charles came yawning downstairs he had only to wait a few minutes, for the telephone was on the other side of the room and somebody was always wanting the sergeant-major on the telephone. As soon as the seat was vacant Charles took leisurely possession of it. He had no regard for the dignity of sergeant-majors.

Many a time I came into the company office to find the C.S.M. standing up and Charles asleep on his chair. When I told the sergeant-major to turn him off, he shook his head. 'No, sir', he said. 'That cat, sir – that cat keeps looking at me when he wants the chair and I haven't the heart.'

Were it not for the fact that no warrant officer in the Queen's Own Royal West Kent Regiment could possibly be frightened of anything, I might have suspected that the sergeant-major was frightened of Charles. It may have been purely fanciful on my part, but it seemed to me that Charles was regarded with awe and admiration among all ranks of the company as a result of this cavalier treatment of the C.S.M.

When it was my duty to dispense justice according to military law I could not help noticing the sidelong looks which defaulters and their escorts gave Charles as he lay blissfully asleep on the sergeant-major's chair or among the once neatly arranged papers on his table. I often wondered what the men were thinking. Was it secret envy of a cat who could thus defy anyone as mighty as a warrant officer? Or was it merely another piece of evidence that their company commander was a bit queer in the head to have such a curious animal as a pet? Anyhow, I am sure that Charles was often discussed among the N.C.O.s and men.

At night Charles always slept on my bed. He was disturbed on many occasions, for the battalion was being frequently rehearsed in taking up action stations during the night. Poor Charles! He must have wondered what all the commotion was about. I had to sleep with one eye open, for we never knew when the next alarm would come through, and it was a race against time to get into battle dress and equipment. Charles took a poor view of these midnight excursions and would miauow protestingly from the bed as he watched my frantic preparations. To him it must have seemed that the world had gone mad, and indeed he was not far wrong.

Even when there was no stand-to during the night the sound of the sentries pacing to and fro outside and the words of command given by guard commanders when the guard was changed were clearly audible, but Charles soon learned that this was ordinary routine and slept through it all.

It was another very hard winter and although Charles contrived to keep warm most of the time and had an abundance of good food, including a regular supply of locally caught rabbits which he particularly relished, he was now beginning to show his age. I could sympathize with him, for now that I was back in the army and coping with the strenuous responsibilities of my job I too had began to realize that I was not so young as I had been. There were fleeting moments when I wished myself back in the easy-going days of peace – but it was no use wishing for that. Charles and I were in the army now.

We did however get occasional glimpses of the rest of the family for when I had a few hours' leave of absence I put Charles in his basket and motored across Dorset to see them. Charles and Rissa were always glad to see each other again and no doubt had plenty of news to exchange. Rissa had settled down happily enough in her temporary home, as I had expected, for she was a self-contained little cat. I left Charles with the family when I went to London on forty-eight hours' leave to participate in a broadcast programme about cats. This caused a good deal of amusement in the battalion and probably set the seal on my reputation for oddity. With a few exceptions I have no doubt that my brother officers thought it evidence of mental instability to prefer cats to dogs, or at any rate to make an exhibition of myself in public on the subject.

It was still bitterly cold, and when the day came for us to leave the beach the roads were frozen and treacherous. We made our way in convoy to our destination in Berkshire, where we were to resume intensive training, as the battalion had been singled out for even more onerous duties.

Charles had viewed our preparations for departure with great dejection. To his way of thinking it was obviously madness to travel in the depth of winter. Galea made his basket as comfortable and warm as possible but he was not to be appeased. My car led the company's transport and it was as well that we were spaced out at intervals along the road, for Charles kept up a continuous howl of protest which did not enhance our military dignity.

We were bound for a small town which in the more spacious days of peace had been a flourishing centre of horse-racing activity. We found on arrival that several stables were still functioning, although their strings of horses were comparatively small. The men of my company were quartered in a yard which in its time had housed two famous Derby winners. My own billet was in a house nearby.

I had been rather anxious about Charles, for now that the rifle company officers were to rejoin the battalion mess I should have to make special arrangements if, as was likely, it was not possible for me to have Charles in my billet. Leonard Olney and another officer were billeted in the same house, and it was Leonard who greeted me with the cheering news that our billet landlady was fond of cats and had no objection to Charles.

This was good news indeed. Charles seemed to know that he had fallen on his feet, for he inspected our new quarters with obvious approval. I was rather taken aback when a majestic tail-less black cat appeared round the corner with an enquiring look on his face. This turned out to be Mrs. Cook's cat Stooky. Far from resenting our intrusion he seemed to welcome it and although a little on his dignity at first he was uncommonly friendly. Charles, I am sorry to say, so far forgot himself as to repulse Stooky's first advances but he soon changed his mind and the two cats became friendly.

Leonard had not exaggerated, I found, when he said that Mrs. Cook was fond of cats. She and her husband and their little daughter Jennifer welcomed Charles as if he had been their own cat, and did everything they could to make him comfortable. He was given the freedom of the house, Mr. Cook allowed him to sit on his knee, Jennifer played with him, Mrs. Cook petted him, everybody fed him; and all the time Stooky looked on benevolently. Stooky was the most hospitable cat I have ever met; and he was handsome and intelligent as well. I am sure it was Stooky who taught Charles that it was silly to be afraid of horses; for Stooky had been brought up among some of the finest racehorses in the world and knew all about them.

During our stay Charles was almost spoiled with kindness. As soon as I had left the house for early morning parade Charles presented himself for breakfast with Mr. and Mrs. Cook. He had porridge, with cream from the top of the milk, and scraps of bacon every morning and I suspect that he had a goodly share of other delicacies from the larder. His kind-hearted hostess made a great fuss of him and Charles thoroughly enjoyed himself.

He had the grace to sleep with me at night, and I learned afterwards that he even deserted Mr. Cook's knee when he heard my returning footsteps: but perhaps that was only his way of showing gratitude for the wonderful place I had brought him to. In addition to all the admiration and material comforts showered on him he also had his great friends Lieutenant Leonard Olney and Private Eric Galea living under the same roof. What more could he desire?

To my great regret the battalion moved again before the end of February. We reluctantly said good-bye to the Cooks, promising to come and see them again at the first opportunity. In spite of the wintry weather it had been the happiest month of Charles's life in the army – of that I am sure.

The battalion went by train to our new area, somewhere in Bedfordshire. Leonard Olney was one of the advance party who went by road and I was thus able to send Charles with him in the car. The billeting arrangements were in the hands of the advance party and when the company arrived at the village we were to occupy, I was faced with a problem.

I was billeted in a large and comfortable house at one end of the village, with company headquarters and the mess at the other end. In my billet lived Mr. and Mrs. Allan Wood, their daughter Mary, two servants, several young evacuees from London and one of their school teachers, Miss Goodwin. That was not all. There was Albert, a stately black cat, and Bogey, a large Airedale terrier. Mrs. Wood, on hearing about Charles, kindly offered to accommodate Charles as well – but there was Bogey. And somehow I did not think Charles would be happy with Bogey, for he was not used to large dogs. And in any case the house was already as full as it could be.

The alternative was to leave Charles at the company officers' mess, in charge of Galea, and this I decided to do. The mess and batmen's quarters were in the wing of a house well off the main Bedford road, and there was plenty of room for Charles. I should be able to see him every day, and Galea would see to it that he was well fed and looked after. It was in many ways an ideal place for Charles, as the house stood on the bank of the river Ouse, and now that spring days were near he would be able to go out for walks as and when he felt like it.

These arrangements however did not turn out at all well. In the first place the weather remained obstinately cold and unpleasant, with snow and rain alternating. I saw little of Charles after the first few days for our training had now reached the stage when we were often out all day on field exercises. I tried to make amends one week-end, when I had a few hours off duty, by fishing with a borrowed rod in the Ouse at the back of the mess; but Charles was only mildly interested in the roach I caught and in disgust I presented the rest of my catch to Albert at my billet.

For some time now I had been feeling far from well. One evening I found myself unable to leave my billet where I had gone to change for dinner and when the medical officer of the battalion arrived, hastily fetched by Leonard Olney, he promptly made arrangements for me to be moved to a nursing home in Bedford. I was there for a week under observation, X-rayed, and then allowed to return to my billet: but it was already clear that my days in the army were numbered.

As soon as I could I went round to the mess to see how Charles was getting on. He had not been at all pleased at what he no doubt considered my neglect in the matter of billeting arrangements, and my absence for a whole week was evidently the last straw. Not only did he show no sign of pleasure at seeing me again but he had, I found, been guilty of flagrant breaches of his customary good behaviour. In inhospitable weather Galea faithfully provided him with a tray covered with ashes, but he had ignored it entirely. This was so unusual for Charles that the only possible explanation was that in this way he registered his disgust at my desertion of him.

I was now excused all duties, and as I saw Charles every day and no longer had to rush away on mysterious military errands he seemed to realize that things had changed for the better. Perhaps he took the view that I had at last come to my senses, and knew better than to leave him in the lurch. Or maybe it was the improvement in the weather, which suddenly changed from snow to spring sunshine. Whatever the cause, Charles was soon his old self again.

Although I was still on the strength of the battalion the M.O. recommended me for sick leave, pending the medical board which would decide my future. He privately assured me that there was little chance of my remaining in the army and in any case, as I was no longer fit for active service, I should have to leave the battalion. So, when the time came for me to go on leave, Charles and I said good-bye to our friends with little hope of seeing them again for a long time. Galea was almost in tears when for the last time he put Charles in his basket.

And so, with the car filled with my kit and Charles in his basket by my side, I set out for Gloucestershire to rejoin my family. Our army days were over.

CHAPTER SEVEN

A long period of leisure now lay ahead. It would be two years, I was told, before I could hope to be really fit again. After my strenuous time in the army – and three months 'on the beach' followed by intensive training in an armoured division had been even more of a strain than I had realized at the time – I was thankful for the prospect of a long rest.

It had many compensations. Although I missed the cheerful companionship I had enjoyed in the army I was now able to stay at home, read some at least of the books I had had no time for in the previous year and generally relax. It was also now possible to look for somewhere for us to live, a problem which had been acutely depressing my wife.

We stayed in Gloucestershire until the middle of May, living in primitive fashion in a small picturesque cottage from which on clear days I could see in the distance the Malvern hills which had been the scene of my army training in the summer of the previous year. The cottage was remotely perched on a steep hill a few miles outside Gloucester and although the scenery was magnificent there were many practical disadvantages. It was now becoming increasingly difficult to buy things in shops; and one of my recollections of our stay in the Cotswolds was the occasional success of our shopping expeditions. Sometimes we returned triumphant with a few packets of cigarettes, fish, newspapers, chocolate and other welcome additions to our rations. And there was a shop in Gloucester which sold unrationed horse meat for cats and dogs. Charles and Rissa, who would have turned up their noses at horse meat in the days of pre-war plenty, were now only too glad to get it.

As the weather became milder I was able to sit out of doors, with Charles and a rug on my knees, admiring the glorious view and, closer at hand, the daffodils and polyanthus in the garden. Charles as usual, was grateful for the sun, but now that I could contemplate him at my leisure the clear light revealed that he was growing old. His eyes were as clear and blue as ever, his voice even more resonant; but his brown paws were beginning to be delicately flecked with grey, and he had a middle-aged paunch, which swayed gently from side to side as he walked. His crumpled ear, although no disfigurement in my eyes, also made him look older, for that too had a greyish tinge.

I noticed that he slept more than formerly, never failing to settle down, preferably on my knee, for at least an hour's nap after lunch. I had been advised to rest as much as possible and whenever I put my feet up Charles jumped on my lap without invitation. At night he slept on my bed, no longer wandering off on mysterious errands as in his early days. He was more affectionate than ever, showing his devotion in a score of different ways: purring continuously, following me about, asking to be taken up and petted, talking to me in the muted, plaintive tones I knew so well. He liked to lick the back of my hand, and I had only to lower my head for him to lick my hair vigorously and with every appearance of delight. He never tired of this and only stopped when I moved away. I used to impress visitors by demonstrating this as a display of Charles's affection but the truth probably is that, like the hedgehog who will climb to lick the plough handle, he was attracted by the saline flavour.

We had to remain near Gloucester until my medical board but when this had been held we moved again. Since I could not return to my office in London and had been advised to remain in the country if possible, we decided to look for a house in Berkshire. We had been offered a short tenancy of a pleasantly furnished house near Wantage, from which it would be convenient to look round for something more permanent.

In June 1941 we found an unfurnished house a few miles from Newbury and, having arranged for our furniture to be moved from London, we took possession. It was a charming farm house, with a pleasant outlook, and I noted with satisfaction that it had central heating. When the cold weather came again Charles would be glad of that.

After so many changes and upheavals Charles may have viewed our new home with mental reservations, but when the remembered furniture was installed and arranged I think he knew this was no temporary lodging. He showed his satisfaction by renewing his old iniquitous habit of scratching the carpets and it was not long before there was another almost bare patch at the top of the stairs. As soon as he knew his way about the house he began to explore outside, with the wariness that life in the country had taught him. I think he missed the London pavements, which he would have preferred to fields and cows and farm buildings; but in spite of the cows which placidly grazed in a neighbouring meadow the new house met with his approval.

A family of cats lived in the farm buildings near by but Charles did not resent their presence. Rissa was much more hostile, taking an instant and never-to-be-relaxed dislike to the black-and-white mother of the family. The black tom was obviously beneath Charles's notice, but no doubt remembering the orange-and-white sultan of his St. John's Wood days, Charles was careful to keep out of his way. Shirley, whose love for cats is all-embracing, at once made friends with the farm cats, and they follow her about to this day. They soon learned to present themselves at the back door early every morning for breakfast. Before the year was out two generations of farm kittens had also learned to parade at regular hours for meals provided by Shirley, much to Rissa's disgust. For the most part the farm cats had hitherto lived on the plentiful rats and mice which infested the farm buildings, eked out with young rabbits in season and whatever one of the men brought to work with him; but now they were in clover.

There was a fairly large and well-kept garden, with an old walnut-tree and a pine-tree on one side of the house, a convenient space on the other side for a hen run, fruit trees, plenty of room to grow our vegetables, and fields all round the house. A family of owls nesting in the walnut-tree terrified Rissa with their screeching and swooping flight to the ground: Charles, who to an owl probably looked too formidable for even simulated attack, was left in peace. There was a great variety of other birds at all seasons: woodpeckers, whose loud tapping aroused Charles's curiosity until he became used to the sound when, as usual, he ignored it completely, chaffinches, hedge-sparrows, rooks, wood-pigeons, tits, bullfinches, blackbirds, jays, robins, magpies, jackdaws and many less familiar birds. At sunset the raucous 'cock up, cock up' cry of roosting pheasants was to be heard in the distance.

It did not take Rissa long to discover that there were rabbits in plenty. She had learned in Gloucestershire that rabbits could be caught, and now she went hunting regularly. Charles looked on wistfully when she came in carrying a young rabbit. Perhaps he was trying to pretend that rabbit-hunting had no attraction for him, but I think he was now too old for sport of that kind. He was content to lie in the sun, indolently watching the birds and butterflies and bees.

For me that first summer at Copyhold Farm was a pleasant experience. I was beginning to feel better, and now for the first time in my life I was able to stay at home and take things easily. After the pressure of army life it was a relief to be able to lie in the sun and do practically nothing. Charles was delighted. He no longer had to wonder where on earth I was off to every morning, nor had he to wait up for me at night and, heaven be praised, I was no longer so foolish as to live among men who inexplicably turned out of their beds in the middle of the night and disappeared among strange oaths and the clatter of military equipment. Now I could be relied upon to stroll out into the garden and lie on a seat in the sun with a cushion under my head and plenty of room for him to go to sleep on top of me.

When autumn came he must have been pleasantly surprised at the warmth of the house. There was no ban then on central heating and Charles's delight must have been unbounded at the discovery that notwithstanding the cold outside there were warm corners all over the house.

He showed his appreciation by establishing his favourite places, carefully chosen not only for their gratifying heat but also for their draught-proof convenience. On really cold days, when the pipes and radiators were not giving out a robust enough heat, he took refuge in the linen cupboard, which could always be relied upon for the maximum of comfort. There were occasional wails from my wife, whose theory was that Charles invariably selected the most delicate and precious linen to lie on, but as Rissa copied Charles in making use of the cupboard, Shirley and I were in a majority in upholding their claim to shelter.

Now that I was home all day I was able, for the first time, to observe Charles in all his moods. He soon adopted a routine of his own, and it seldom varied. If the weather looked unpromising he was reluctant to get up. Occasionally, if he had business of his own to attend to he would get up early but he nearly always awaited the arrival of my breakfast tray. It was his privilege to be given a little milk in my saucer and I am sure that he often drank it more for the sake of ceremony than because he was thirsty. He was not a great lover of milk. I usually had a very light breakfast but sometimes there was fish, and on those mornings he gave me no peace, stretching out an appealing paw until I gave him his share. Having breakfasted, he would curl up on the end of my bed and go to sleep again.

I had volunteered to do certain domestic chores, among them the making of beds, which (like making tea) I had for years insisted that no woman could do efficiently. I was indulged in this fanciful theory, no doubt because in a servant-less household any help was welcome. At any rate I made up two of the beds. There were mornings when I postponed the job as long as possible, in order not to disturb my sleeping cat; and it was an understanding between us that I should always make my wife's bed before my own. Charles pretended to be asleep, but he knew perfectly well that when I reached the stage of putting on her counterpane it was time for him to get up. Then he would stretch and yawn himself into proper wakefulness and jump off my bed without haste, as though he had intended to get up at that very moment. But I knew, and he knew, that he timed his departure to avoid the indignity of being removed.

His first port of call was the kitchen, to see if there was anything exciting in the dishes which were kept in a corner near the larder door. Then, if the weather permitted, he would stroll outside to inspect his domain, one eye always open for the black tom-cat. Sometimes he followed me about as I went to refill the coke scuttles or to look at the garden. I was allowed to look after the pansies and spent a good deal of time removing the dead flowers. I liked to count them as I did so, taking pleasure in collecting a basketful of several hundred dead blooms: and Charles at least was tolerant of this ridiculous habit. On sunny days he would lie on the warm earth, his blue eyes sleepily following me as I worked my way down the long row of flowers. To his way of thinking this was a more sensible occupation than such activities as chopping logs, with their menace of flying splinters.

If I felt energetic I would do something to the car, and while I did so it was one of Charles's privileges to be allowed inside. He was happily at ease lying on the warm upholstery. Even on sunless days the inside of the car was sheltered and comparatively warm, and he often installed himself there.

He was also privileged to go to sleep on my desk. This was one of his best loved places, for the morning sun shone directly on to it. He liked to squeeze himself between my typewriter and the tray containing my papers. I had to keep them in a tray, for otherwise I should have found them scattered all over the floor as often as not. I used my desk regularly during the autumn of 1941, as I was writing a book about my experiences in the army. It was dedicated when finished, 'To Charles O'Malley, Comrade in Arms.'

The typewriter interested him enormously. In the past I had rarely used a typewriter, preferring to write with a pen, but to save paper I now tried the experiment of typing my work. Whether I used a pen or a machine, Charles was fascinated. The gentle scratch of a nib and the rustle of paper engaged his solemn attention and the clatter and tinkle of the typewriter aroused his intent curiosity. But after a while he would give up trying to discover what made the bell ring and would settle down to sleep, usually in an inconvenient place.

I never disturbed him unless it was absolutely necessary, for I found his company very much to my liking. If I were stuck for a word I sometimes put a question to him, when he would open one sleepy eye, with the air of one who says, with tranquil wisdom, 'What does it matter? One word or another, it's all the same to me, and I dare say to everybody else.'

If I had to remove him bodily from my desk, as I did occasionally, telling him sharply that he took up too much room, he would yawn politely and transfer himself to the window ledge and curl up next to my yellow china cat Eustace. There were times, of course, when I played truant and in such moods, when I found writing more than usually laborious, I would do anything to avoid going on with my self-imposed task. The easiest way of escape was to crumple up a ball of paper and throw it across the room. That would awaken Charles in an instant. He liked nothing better than to scamper after a paper ball. Or I would turn him over on his back on the floor and gently place my foot on his white belly fur. That was the signal for a determined assault on my intruding foot with his strong back legs, which kicked out convulsively while he pretended to bite with his teeth. He assumed an expression of ogre-like ferocity while this was going on and when I finally released him he continued to scowl and lash his tail wildly. But he spoiled the effect by purring loudly at the same time.

I could always tempt him to play, but most of the time he liked to spend resting: outside in the sun, in the house in patches of sunlight; near the hot-water pipes or radiators if there was no sun; in the linen cupboard when it was really cold. Food was highly important, and when he knew there was something tasty in the larder he presented himself at frequent intervals in the kitchen, looking as hungry and forlorn as possible. He made full use of his clamorous voice, which became most appealing when Shirley or I passed through the kitchen. Rissa, having no voice of her own except an almost inaudible chirrup, often made use of Charles by stationing herself at his side when he proclaimed his hunger. His voice was insistent enough for two.

After lunch both cats settled down for their siesta, and it was part of Charles's routine to take his nap on my knee. No other cat would have submitted to so many interruptions. Again and again I moved him to go and look up a word or a quotation as I struggled

97

with my daily crossword puzzle. I read many manu-
scripts while resting, but Charles slept on beneath the
weight of their pages. Against doctor's orders I smoked
a great deal and that, too, must have been a grave discomfort to Charles, who shared the dislike of all cats
for cigarette smoke. But he endured all these inconven-
iences. I like to think he preferred my knee to the
warmth of the linen cupboard but perhaps it was
merely part of his cherished routine. It is at any rate
true to say that he had only to see me put my feet up
on the couch to leave the fireside or wherever he was
and establish himself on my lap.

The best time was the evening. We rarely had visitors and Charles could count on an undisturbed
routine. I read a book or manuscript, sitting or lying on
the couch, listened to the wireless, or played the piano.
Charles was seldom more than a yard or two away.
Sometimes I played patience, under difficulties, for
Charles found playing-cards alluring and liked to lie
on them.

Now that we were living in the country we went
early to bed, and it was never too early for Charles. It
was my custom to carry him upstairs, for now that he
was older I no longer perched him on my shoulder,
although he was always willing to stay there. He liked
being carried about and would lie in my arms completely relaxed and comfortable. This was in agreeable
contrast to Rissa, who could not bear to be picked up
and would struggle furiously to be released if anyone
tried to carry her. While I was carrying him he closed
one of his paws round my finger, the soft pads of his

foot encircling and the outstretched claws holding tightly on to the end of the finger: this too was part of his nightly routine. If I went upstairs without him I could be sure that he would follow me, entering the bedroom with an aggrieved expression and gentle reproach in his muted voice.

He omitted no part of the bed-time ceremonial. Until I began to undress he sat contentedly on the end of the bed or on an armchair, but as soon as I had taken off my shoes he rubbed himself against them and my legs as energetically as ever. It was still asking for trouble to walk about in bare feet and I usually remembered not to expose my feet to his playful attacks. But if I incautiously did so he would rush at them pretending to bite and scratch in the traditional manner.

As soon as I was in bed – and if I took a long time about it Charles would remind me of the necessity of keeping to time-table by jumping on the bed himself – he had his own method of settling down. I always read in bed, and he used to wait until I was comfortably settled. Then he would stealthily approach me, always from the same side, climb to my chest, and start purring as loudly as he could. I often pretended I did not want him but that made no difference. He insinuated himself with great determination into the desired position. And there he would lie, purring his pleasure until it was time for me to put away my book or paper, switch off the light, and turn over to go to sleep.

There were usually rusks in a tin I kept by the side of my bed. Rusks met with Charles's approval and although he found it rather difficult to eat them with his teeth, which had given him trouble in recent years, he always asked for his share. This meant that I had to break up one small rusk into manageable pieces, put them on a newspaper and hand them over. It was sometimes quite obvious that he was not hungry but he always insisted on his portion. It was one of his many small privileges.

The winter of 1941 was again very cold, and we had long periods of snow. Charles had a visible hatred of snow, although he hated the cold wind and rain even more. He still asked to be let out but when the door was opened he bristled with annoyance, recoiling on the threshold as though he had been ordered to walk the plank. Then he summoned up his courage and made a dash for it. Against the white background of the snow his coat was the colour of a dirty blanket. While snow was on the ground, and at one time that winter it was a foot deep outside the house, his indignation was intense. It was as much as I could do not to laugh outright as he tried with a series of quivering jerks to shake his feet free from the clogging snow.

He was a different cat in winter. He seemed to swell visibly when he went out of doors, puffing out his fur, as birds do their feathers, as a protection against the cold. I saw to it that his tray was always ready for him, for he was now too old a cat to be turned outside in bad weather; but he insisted on going out in spite of his aversion to cold and rain and snow. If he found the doors closed against him when he wanted to come in he wasted no time trying to make himself heard outside the front or back door, but jumped on the narrow sloping outside ledge of the drawing-room window or stood up against the windows of my own room which were within a foot of the ground outside, his paws scraping at the glass until he was let in. The noise of my typewriter often brought both cats to my room: they knew they could count on my opening the window without delay, summer or winter, if they wanted to come in.

Before winter had really set in that year, Charles had another trial to endure. Eleanor Farjeon wrote to ask me if I knew anyone who would adopt a young Siamese cat, whose owner expected to be called up at short notice for war work. There is something irresistible about Eleanor Farjeon's letters and with misgivings I found myself wondering, since I knew at that time no suitable home for the cat, whether we dared add her to our own household. It was true that the cats were used to newcomers – but a Siamese? That was something which might well break Charles's heart. I pondered briefly on the problem, rashly mentioned it to Shirley, and then had no peace until I had written to Eleanor Farjeon to say that I should be delighted to offer a home to her young friend's Siamese, Madame Emma Bovary.

Shirley and I met Emma at the station and carried her home in triumph. She was a beautiful cat, with true Siamese features, and showed no sign of alarm at being conducted to her new home. At first we mistook her demeanour for well-bred reticence: only later were we to discover that Emma was the most self-possessed and brazen cat we had ever met.

For my part, I was now full of apprehension. What would Charles say to this newcomer: one of his own clan, destined (I could well imagine him instantly thinking) to inherit his unique place in my affection? It was with considerable trepidation that we introduced Emma into the drawing-room, where Charles and Rissa were sitting peaceably by the fire.

To my great relief there was no ill-mannered outburst. Charles stared, perhaps unbelievingly, at the slim, elegant creature: Rissa, her eyes bright and suspicious, retreated to the other side of the room. Only Emma was unperturbed. She condescendingly made her way to the middle of the hearth-rug, stared back at Charles, gave Rissa a look of social discouragement – and settled down to enjoy the warmth of the fire. A few minutes later she had the temerity to play with Charles's tail. I can only think that he was speechless and paralysed with astonishment, for he made no move to put her in her place.

From that moment Madame Emma Bovary took possession of the house. She treated Charles and Rissa with serene indifference, provided they had the good sense to give her pride of place. She sat nearest the fire, stole their food, appropriated their favourite chairs and corners, and generally behaved as if they were cats of no account. Nothing disconcerted her: not even my refusal to have her on my knee in place of Charles. She even strolled into my bedroom and seeing Charles on the end of my bed, or sensing that he was there, boldly jumped up as though she expected the same preferential treatment.

During this first phase, when our two cats were so taken aback that they hardly knew how to retaliate or even defend their rights, Emma was a constant source of surprise. She, a cat who had lived all her life in a London flat, took to the country as a duck takes to water. She made friends with the farm cats, shared their meals – her appetite was prodigious – and explored the surrounding barns and fields with the possessive interest of one who has newly inherited some valuable property. She disdained the tray I provided for her toilet, preferring to go out of doors in all weathers. She caught rats as large as herself in the neighbouring farm buildings, arousing the admiration of the oldest farm hand, who informed us in broad Berkshire that he never see a cat like 'un. She went into the woods and brought back more rabbits than Rissa and the farm cats caught between them. Charles looked on, indifferently. He was like Mark Twain's cat Tom Quartz, who 'never ketched a rat in his life – 'peared to be above it.'

Indoors Emma was irrepressible. I tried to teach her that it was Charles's exclusive privilege to sit on my knee, but she was not to be snubbed. She took a perverse delight in occupying the central place on the drawing-room hearth-rug, thus depriving the other cats of the warmest place in the room. Charles pretended not to mind and usually took refuge on my knee or the arm of a chair, but Rissa stood her ground, staring malevolently at this ill-mannered new-comer.

But it was impossible not to like Emma in spite of her egotism. She was affectionate and intelligent. She was beautiful and graceful. No true gardener ever loves cats but even Edna admired her courage and resourcefulness. In time, we hoped, mutual tolerance would develop into a happier relationship, and all three cats would settle down together.

Meanwhile, in January of that winter, Charles's other ear began to trouble him. He had for a long time been afflicted with ear trouble, and when haematoma set in there was nothing for it but another operation. We were now too far away to go to Bryan Cartland, but fortunately there was a good veterinary surgeon in Newbury. I left Charles with him for a few days, after which I dressed the ear myself. It took some time to heal and Charles cried dolefully when he saw me making preparations for another dressing. But he lay patiently and quietly on a cushion in my room while I attended to him, painful though the treatment must have been: and he never failed to show his relief and thanks when the ordeal was over. He knew that it was necessary, and that I had been as gentle as I could.

When he was well again his appearance was certainly improved, for he now had two crumpled ears instead of one. I agreed with Shirley that he had recovered his good looks, although to the inexperienced eye he no doubt looked as sinister as ever. The patch of fur between his ears had grown lighter, partly as a result of the frequent applications of peroxide of hydrogen, and that too improved his general appearance.

CHAPTER EIGHT

As the days grew longer and winter merged into spring Charles again renewed his youth. He was surprisingly active for his age, and his delight in the sun was as keen as ever. His appetite was undiminished and it was fortunate that we lived in the country, for we could occasionally get rabbits and game; and although Charles had never learned to catch rabbits there were few things he liked better to eat. Indeed he fared very well, considering that we were living under conditions of increasing austerity.

Emma and Rissa were now in their element, with baby rabbits to be had everywhere in the woods. Emma earned good marks from my wife by catching (although she never attempted to eat them) a number of young moles which were busy undermining the best part of our lawn. Charles, as was to be expected, showed no interest in moles, but one evening I picked up a young hedgehog and brought it into the house. This did interest him. I doubt if he had ever seen a hedgehog before, for since we had lived in the country he seldom went exploring at night. He inspected the prickly ball with every sign of curiosity but showed some alarm when the little creature uncoiled itself. Stationing himself at a discreet distance he watched with evident surprise while the hedgehog drank milk from a saucer. The hedgehog, not in the least perturbed by Charles's presence, advanced towards him. This was too much for Charles, who fled. He would not come back until he was satisfied I had put the hedgehog out of doors where he belonged.

Another surprise was in store for Charles, for at about that time Shirley had her own way once more and bought a young goat. Like most people who had never had anything to do with goats I had the idea that goats are uninteresting animals. But I soon found out how wrong I was.

Amelia was a hornless British Toggenburg, a pretty little thing with white markings and two tassels hanging from her neck. She was a most engaging animal, high-spirited and playful, and soon became very friendly. When she first saw Charles she made it clear that she was quite ready for a game. By this time one would have thought that Charles would not have been surprised at anything which found its way into our domestic menagerie but Milly (as she was soon called, Amelia having been found too formal) terrified him. He crouched on the grass well out of her reach and made off as soon as he decently could. It was several days before he could be persuaded to go anywhere near her.

However great his fear of anything strange, Charles's curiosity always obliged him to make a careful inspection before beating a retreat. And as soon as he was satisfied that he would not come to any harm he was tolerant enough of other animals. He was now familiar with such phenomena as cows and horses and, no doubt thanks to his tail-less friend Stooky of Lambourn, he showed no fear of Shirley's pony Simon when she brought him up to the house. Simon was stabled some distance away and Charles saw him only at intervals. To the unenlightened eye, seeing Charles crouching a few yards away, it might have appeared that he was frightened of the lively young chestnut, but I could see that he was only on the look-out in case Simon broke loose from the wall at the back of the house where he was tethered. Fortunately Charles was not about on the day that Shirley ventured to bring her pony into the kitchen for that I am sure would have caused trouble. Charles believed in keeping four-legged visitors in their place.

Milly, with her playful antics at the end of a taut rope, was more formidable than any horse, but presently Charles realized that she could only perform in a strictly limited radius. A few inches beyond her reach he knew he was safe, and it was amusing to watch him as he dozed in the sunshine or cleaned his paws as though she did not exist. But when it was warm enough to have the garden seat out there were complications, for Milly took an instant fancy to the seat and would lie down on it whenever she had the chance. And the garden seat was part of Charles's property.

So long as I was there with him he was very still, lying on my knee like a hare in its form; but he did not like it at all when Milly poked her nose in as he slept on the cushions alone. At first he surrendered the seat without ceremony but after a time his courage, or rather his dignity, returned; and although he sat stiffly resenting Milly's playful advances he would not give up his place.

We had added some ducklings to our hens, and whether it was because they were about the same size as the hens and were associated in his mind with them, or because he had seen them grow from ducklings into ducks, Charles had no fear of them. They were for a time allowed the run of the garden and they waddled all over the place, loudly quacking. Charles simply ignored them.

Nor did he take much notice of the house martins which regularly nest at Copyhold Farm. One of the sunniest places in the house was the top of a chest of drawers which stood against a window upstairs, and the martins' nest was in the eaves, only a few feet away. Even when the window was open Charles merely watched the birds with idle curiosity as he lay basking in the sun. The Staffordshire china was indeed in greater peril than the martins, and my wife often feared for its safety. He did in fact knock over one or two pieces when he made a more than usually clumsy jump, but they were fairly large and came to no harm; and I put them back before Edna could see them.

Rissa and Emma behaved very differently. It was chiefly on their account that this particular window was usually kept shut, for although they could both be relied upon to steer miraculously clear of the china the martins would have been in danger. Rissa in particular was often to be found on top of the chest, closely watching the birds as they entered and left the nest and lashing her tail in exasperation at the closed window. Emma was usually on some more productive errand. She could often be seen from one of the windows upstairs, crouching near a rabbit warren at the edge of the woods patiently waiting.

Emma had her first kittens in May: five lusty, plebeian black kittens. There was no doubt about their paternity, for apart from their striking resemblance to the black tom-cat, we had observed with varying degrees of amusement the domestic comedy that took place in and around the garden and the adjacent farm buildings. Before Emma's arrival the two farm cats were the very pattern of matrimonial bliss. Shirley had pointed out that they were just like a Victorian husband and wife, taking their morning promenade together and sitting side by side on the sunny side of the nearest haystack. It was only a question of time before Emma, who had inveigled herself into their family circle, assumed the rôle of the other woman. To our surprise the female farm cat did not object. Indeed she was quite complacent about her husband's goings-on and continued to favour Emma with her friendship.

Now that Emma had kittens to look after she was hungrier than ever; and as they grew up she brought in young rabbits daily, teaching the kittens how to eat them. Emma's notion of eating rabbits was to consume everything except odd bits of fur, and the kittens enthusiastically followed her example. She was immensely proud of her kittens although they in no way resembled her. There was not a visible trace of Siamese in their appearance.

It was, I believe, the arrival of her kittens which destroyed our hope that Emma would settle down harmoniously with our two cats. Where she had been pert and acquisitive before she now became positively aggressive, and Charles and Rissa were given no peace. It became increasingly obvious that something would have to be done about it; and when I heard of a farmer's wife who was a cat-lover and wanted a cat, especially when she heard it was a Siamese, I reluctantly decided that we should have to let Emma go. Her kittens had grown up and been given away and this was an opportunity not to be missed. We did not flatter ourselves that Emma would mourn our society, for there never was a cat so independent and self-reliant. Yet I hated to part with her. I have no doubt she is happy, queening it in her own territory and, if I am not mistaken, living on the fat of the land, even in war-time.

With her departure Charles and Rissa were able to resume their peaceable routine, and I am sure they did so with gratitude.

Now that I was living at home I took much more notice of Rissa than I had ever done before. She had always been Shirley's cat but Shirley was preoccupied for much of her time with her pony and Milly, who followed her like a dog whenever she went for a walk. It gradually became an accepted domestic convention that I should call Rissa by another name and thus acquire proprietorial rights. So Rissa became 'Lucy' to me and Shirley acquiesced, more or less gracefully, in the arrangement.

This did not disturb Charles, for he knew that my benevolent interest in Rissa did not detract in any way from my unique affection for him: and, as always, the two cats were the best of friends. When I yielded to 'Lucy's' occasional blandishments and had her on my knee for a few moments he would eye me with a mildly reproachful look. But he bore no malice and would always take her place as soon as she had left it. Perhaps it was an understanding between them that she should not stay with me for long.

That summer passed all too quickly. Charles was content to lie at ease in the sun and except for the flies, which we both hated, I think it was the happiest time of his life. We had been at Copyhold Farm for a year, and there were no signs of another move; not even preparations for an annual family holiday. The suitcases and trunks were all buried away. Sometimes I went to London for the day but I think he could tell from the family conversation that I was expected to return in a short time. Food was plentiful, and much to his liking. Best of all, he could count on day after day of undisturbed routine.

But in the bright sunlight I could see that he was ageing fast. He had a grey look about him and his movements, though still graceful, were more deliberate. He walked slowly across the grass, and slept more than ever. He was still ready to play and I could always tempt him. But he was no longer a young cat.

These were physical signs. In other ways he was the same affectionate and intelligent cat, always responsive to my mood. He was a cat of acute perceptions. He knew at once when I was melancholy or depressed, and had his own ways of comforting me. If I were in a bad temper he was silent and unobtrusive, waiting for my evil mood to pass. When I was cheerful and ready for play, so was he. There were days when I had to stay in bed, and then he rarely left me. Not even the glowing sun outside could lure him from my room.

His devotion when he knew that something was amiss with me moved me deeply. I was intermittently ill during the summer and in the autumn I had to remain in bed for about a fortnight. During that time Charles never left me except to go out on his lawful occasions, or to eat; and he was never away for long. My doctor smiled indulgently when he saw Charles lying on my bed.

I had for some time been dreading, on Charles's account the coming winter; and I think I must have had a premonition of his death, for my wife will bear witness that I spoke several times of his not surviving the winter which was fast approaching. I believe that Charles too knew that his end was near, for he seemed to want to stay with me all the time. At night, when I slept badly, he did his best to comfort me, licking my hand to show his sympathy, and lying as close to me as he could.

When I was up and about again a sudden spell of cold weather descended on us. There was an official ban on central heating that autumn and Edna considerately made room in the linen cupboard for the cats. Both Charles and Rissa spent much of their time there. No doubt they wondered when we were going to make the pipes and radiators hot again, but they enjoyed the freedom of the linen cupboard until it was possible to use the central heating, luxuriously occupying the shelf that had been reserved for them.

One morning early in December I knew there was something wrong with Charles. He followed me into the bathroom, which he had not done for a long time, and sat under the hot towel rail while I had my bath. When I spoke to him he looked up at me with sadness in his eyes, and only the faintest sound came from him. I looked at him more closely. When I saw that his breathing was irregular I telephoned Addis in Newbury.

When Mr. Kefford came he found that Charles's temperature was slightly above normal. There were indications of bronchitis and tonsillitis. Charles must be kept indoors, he said, out of draughts, and he would send a bottle of friar's balsam and some pills from Newbury.

The next day Charles seemed no worse, although he would not eat. That did not surprise me, for even slight indisposition always put him off his food. In the night, when I was lying awake, I heard a faint squeaking noise which sounded like mice in the wainscot. Charles heard it too and jumped off the bed to investigate. It was a good sign. The following morning there was a definite improvement. Charles drank a little milk, ate a few morsels of rabbit and seemed much more cheerful. When Mr. Kefford arrived and took his temperature he purred. That may have been because he liked his new doctor, who dealt so gently with him when his ear had had to be treated and who now handled him with expert kindness.

The temperature was down to normal. 'Give the pills a chance,' said Kefford, 'but his breathing is not laboured now; so don't bother with the friar's balsam.'

Giving pills to Charles was something I always hated, for in my anxiety not to hurt or frighten him I usually made a mess of the job. It looks so simple when you see a skilled veterinary surgeon put a pill on a cat's tongue, gently close the mouth on it and stroke the throat downwards to assist the passage of the pill. When I tried it the pill somehow found its way to the side of or under the tongue, and would be spat out as soon as Charles could conveniently get rid of it. But I persevered, and although Charles resisted my clumsy efforts I think he knew I was trying to cure him.

The next day Charles again refused all food. His breathing was no longer irregular but he sat quietly on my bed or in one of his favourite corners. Except for his loss of appetite there seemed little wrong with him, and I was not unduly alarmed. That night he jumped on my bed as usual, and slept peacefully.

He was still rather subdued the next day but he drank some water. To outward appearances he was recovering. That afternoon the sun was shining and I went out for a walk. When I came back, it was to hear that Charles had seemed distressed, and had been lying stretched out on the landing.

I went up at once. He was then sitting in his favourite corner, by the hot-water pipe at the back of the chest of drawers from which he had so often watched the martins darting in and out of their nest. He purred when I stroked him. If he was really ill he was making no fuss or complaint. An hour later I carried him downstairs to give him his pill, and then I saw that he was worse. He lay listlessly in my arms, and the lightness of him frightened me. He seemed to have lost weight very suddenly.

I put him gently down on a cushion in front of the fire and he began to cough silently, his tongue hanging out. I hurried to get a kettle of boiling water for the friar's balsam. When I returned a few minutes later he was behind the curtains of the french windows. I picked him up and he lay still in my arms, his jaw sagging. As gently as I could I put him in his basket, which I had put on a chair over the steaming kettle. He rose feebly to his feet, turned round twice, and laid down as if to sleep. But I knew it was no ordinary sleep. My little cat was dead.

* * * * *

'When the day comes for Bunny or Coney to break my heart again,' Eleanor Farjeon wrote to me, 'I shall tell myself this – for more than nine years I have been able to give to a living thing I love the most perfect life

115

possible for a cat to have. It is something that, with all our hearts and wills, we cannot do for our children, whose growing-up and discovery of life is beyond all our longing to keep them happy. You can tell yourself that for nearly thirteen years all Charles's needs of love and care and comfort were perfectly filled by you. . . There will always be other beloved ones of the Company for you to give to and take from, but I know how even that Company is a hierarchy in which some stand higher for us than others.'

Higher for us than others. It is so. For me there will never be another cat like Charles. With him I came nearer than I have ever been, or shall be, to bridging the gulf which divides us from the so-called dumb animals. Many of my happiest hours were spent in his company, for there was communion between us. He tried, as I did, to bridge the gulf; and I do not think I deceive myself if I say that there were times when we came very near to it.

He was a faithful and gentle cat. For kindness and respect he returned an abundant love. I count myself well rewarded for any gentleness he had at my hands.

In the exquisite memorial he wrote for his cat Feathers, Carl Van Vechten wrote, 'It is seemingly very simple, such a companionship, depending on scarcely more than mere propinquity, a few actions, a touch of the cold, moist nose, a soft paw against the cheek, a greeting at the door, a few moments of romping, a warm, soft ball of fur curled on the knee, or a long stare. It is thus that the sympathy between men and animals expresses itself, but inter-woven, and collectively, these details create an emotion which it is **very** difficult even for time to destroy.'

In the midst of a devastating war with all its widespread human suffering the death of a cat may seem an unimportant matter. Those who are indifferent to animals or merely tolerate them will doubtless think so, but anyone who has intimately known and loved an animal and has been honoured with that animal's friendship and devotion will, I believe, agree with me that it is not easy to bear the loss. We must leave it at that.

Charles lies buried in a quiet corner of a Berkshire garden, warmed by the sun. I like to think of him in celestial sunshine, among the honoured cats of all time, exchanging views – who knows? – with Dr. Johnson's Hodge on the relative merits of rusks and oysters. And, as I think of him, I find it easy to agree with Bernard Shaw's Androcles that a heaven in which there are no animals would be a poor place indeed.

TO A SIAMESE CAT

(June 1930–December 1942)

I shall walk in the sun alone
Whose golden light you loved:
I shall sleep alone
And, stirring, touch an empty place:
I shall write uninterrupted
(Would that your gentle paw
Could stay my moving pen just once again!).

I shall see beauty
But none to match your living grace:
I shall hear music
But not so sweet as the droning song
With which you loved me.

I shall fill my days
But I shall not, cannot forget:
Sleep soft, dear friend,
For while I live you shall not die.

M.J.